Critical Praise for Russell Dunn's Guidebooks

Dunn has visited more than 320 waterfalls described in the book,
return
descri
Assoc

Catski

Dunn's ... ry
on each ... in
the car, ... y

A must- ... re
house of ... s

This bo ... of
appealin ... r-
esting h ... e

Adiron

Many of ... le
to catar ... e

If you lov ... .
[It is] a ... n
the easte

... r

This boo ... d
with grac ... y
prompt u

It is the e ... t
about A ... h
places to ... o
small thi ... l

Hudson

Will very likely open eyes to a world of the outdoors that would have
passed us by otherwise. **Times Union**

Those who pick up this extraordinary waterfall guide by Russell
... numerous paths to these and other inspirational places
in the Valley. **Ned Sullivan, president, Scenic Hudson**

Trails with Tales (co-written with Barbara Delaney)

Even if you don't plan on taking the hikes, the book offers Dunn's always-entertaining descriptions of each destination's significance, making it a prime candidate for any history lover's bookshelf.

Hudson Valley

To find such a wide and eclectic variety between the covers of one book, and also within an easy drive of home, is a wonderful gift.

Karl Beard, National Park Service

As a reference tool, it is excellent. … the historical insight gives local hikers a broader understanding and appreciation of the land under their feet. **Times Herald-Record**

This is a refreshing twist on the traditional guidebook. **Adirondac**

Mohawk Region Waterfall Guide

This is the latest in a series of waterfall guides written by Russell Dunn that I recommend to anyone interested in gems which are often overlooked by the public. … Dunn writes in a lucid style with plenty of historical data and anecdotes which make the guide interesting as just plain reading. **The Long Path North News**

Like its predecessors, the guide is well-organized and thoroughly researched. In addition to his field work, he calls on a large, varied selection of books, magazines and newspapers. … Whether you read his books or hear him speak, Dunn will leave you smarter and more appreciative than before of local places, streams, waterfalls and landscapes. **Schenectady Daily Gazette**

Following his successful guides to waterfalls in the Adirondacks, Catskills, and Hudson Valley, Russell Dunn continues with a plethora of falls to explore in the Mohawk region. Again, he does so in a literate, fact-filled fashion with anecdotes and historical data to draw one to these sites. **Adirondac**

Catskill Region
Waterfall
Guide

Cool Cascades of the
Catskills & Shawangunks

Russell Dunn

BLACK·DOME

Published by

Black Dome Press Corp.
1011 Route 296, Hensonville, New York 12439
www.blackdomepress.com
Tel: (518) 734-6357

First Edition Paperback 2004

Library of Congress Cataloging-in-Publication Data

Dunn, Russell.
    Catskill region waterfall guide: cool cascades of the Catskills &
Shawangunks/by Russell Dunn.— 1st ed. pbk.
        p. cm.
    Includes bibliographical references and index.
    ISBN 1-883789-43-5 (alk. paper)

1. Hiking—New York (State)—Catskill Mountains—Guidebooks.
2. Hiking—New York (State)—Shawangunk Mountains—Guidebooks.
3. Automobile travel—New York (State)—Catskill Mountains—Guidebooks.
4. Automobile travel—New York (State)—Shawangunk Mountains—
Guidebooks. 5. Waterfalls—New York (State)—Catskill Mountains—
Guidebooks. 6. Waterfalls—New York (State)—Shawangunk Mountains—
Guidebooks. 7. Catskill Mountains (N.Y.)—Guidebooks. 8. Shawangunk
Mountains (N.Y.)—Guidebooks. I. Title.
    GV199.42.N652C372 2004
    917.47'380444--dc22

                                            2004017062

**Outdoor recreational activities are by their very nature
potentially hazardous and contain risk. See "Safety First," page 17**

The maps in this book were created using TOPO! Interactive Maps
from National Geographic Maps. To learn more about digital
map products from National Geographic Maps, please visit
www.Nationalgeographic.com/topo

Cover photograph: *Upper Kaaterskill Falls,* by David Slutzky.

Design: Ron Toelke Associates

Printed in the USA

        10   9   8   7   6   5   4   3

DISCARDED

Dedicated

to my father,

Cecil G. Dunn,

who as a physicist

taught me how

to both wonder

and be skeptical.

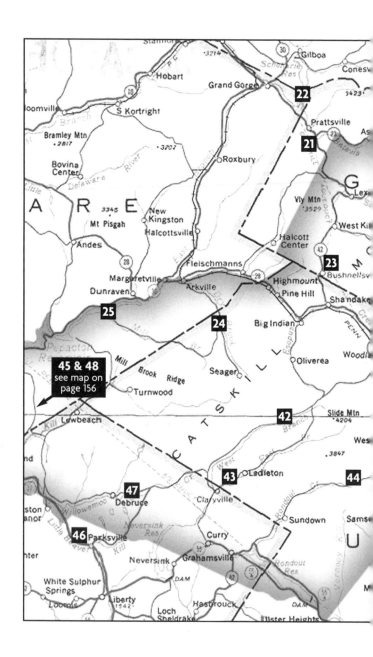

45 & 48
see map on
page 156

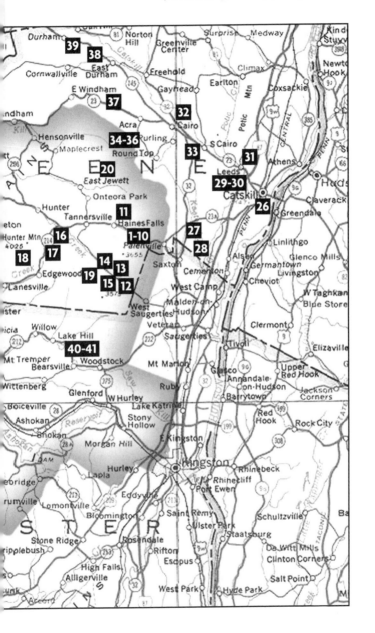

Waterfalls of the Catskills Map Key

Near Palenville

1. Falls in Sleepy Hollow Notch
2. Fall on Lucus Kill

Palenville

3. Roadside Waterfall Tour, including Falls at Tannery Bridge, Ferndale Falls, Niobe Falls, & Helena Falls
4. Palenville Overlook

Kaaterskill Clove

5. Moore's Bridge Falls
6. Fawn's Leap
7. Falls along South Rim, including Viola, Wildcat, Buttermilk, and Santa Cruz Falls
8. Naiad's Bath, The Five Cascades and Haines Falls

Lake Creek Area

9. Bastion Falls
10. Kaaterskill Falls
11. Ashley Falls

Platte Clove

12. Schalk's Falls
13. Hell's Hole
14. Old Mill Falls
15. Plattekill Falls

Stony Clove

16. Fall in Becker Hollow
17. Falls in Stony Notch
18. Diamond Notch Falls
19. Falls on the Roaring Kill
20. **Fall on the East Kill**

Near Prattsville

21. Red Falls
22. Hardenbergh Falls

Near Margaretville

23. Bushnellville Creek Falls
24. Dry Brook Falls
25. Tompkins Falls

Catskill/Leeds Area

26. Klein's Falls
27. Fall on High Falls Road Extension
28. High Falls
29. Falls at Austin Glen
30. Rip Van Winkle Falls
31. Buttermilk Falls

Cairo Area

32. Falls at Woodstock Dam
33. Shingle Kill Falls

Round Top Area

34. Glen Falls
35. Artist Falls
36. Winter Clove Falls

Durham Area

37. Falls in South Durham
38. Fall in East Durham
39. Falls at Zoom Flume (Rumble-Tumble & Shimmering Falls)

Woodstock Area

40. Falls on Sawkill
41. Falls on Tannery Brook

Frost Valley Area

42. High Falls
43. Round Pond Falls
44. **Falls along Peekamoose Road**

Along Route 17

45. Fall in Ferndale (See p.156)
46. Fall in Parksville
47. Falls on Tributary to Willowemoc Creek
48. Russell Brook Falls (See p.156)

Note: shaded area on the map indicates boundaries of the Catskill Park

Table of Contents

Stony Clove as it looked in the early 1900s.

Acknowledgments

Heartfelt thanks to: Barbara Delaney for creating the maps in this book using TOPO! software (and, coincidentally, for being my wife and co-adventurer); Chuck Gibson for permission to use poem "Seven" from his book, *Forty Falls;* Joe Zoske for permission to use his poem, "Waterfalls"; Ralph Keating for several excellent suggestions regarding content; Bob Drew for postcard contributions and for consultation on Lake Minnewaska's history; and Michael A. Larison for information on the Frost Valley YMCA and High Falls.

Special thanks to my editor, Steve Hoare—the wizard behind the curtain—whose judicious, but deft wordsmanship makes me sound good; and boundless thanks to my publisher, Deborah Allen, whose imprint is everywhere in this book. I am grateful to Arthur G. Adams for bringing to bear his encyclopedic knowledge of the Catskill Region in reviewing the contents of this book, and to Edward G. Henry for adding his insights as a conservation professional in his excellent foreword. Additional thanks for the careful eyes and discerning judgment of proofreaders Matina Billias, Natalie Mortensen, and Ed Volmar, and to Ron Toelke Associates for such an attractively designed book.

Postcard illustrations are from the author's collection.

Foreword

Waterfall: the word itself holds special meaning for almost everyone. Waterfalls call to our emotions. Just the mention of the word inspires thoughts of peace, freedom, happiness, eternity, calm, solitude, energy, power and reflection. Visiting a waterfall is always a special event as these vigorous sites soothe our bodies as well as our spirits. We see the tumbling white waters and imposing cliffs, hear the rushing pulses, feel the cool, damp air and misty spray, smell and taste the moisture in the air.

Heading to a waterfall is always a special outing. Listening for the first rush of plunging water and looking for the diving streams are the essence of anticipation when approaching a fall. Russell Dunn's guide enhances this anticipation, as his book flows with the grace of a Catskill cascade, bringing readers to some of the most invigorating and inspiring falls in eastern New York.

New York's southeastern ridges and mountains provide some of the world's best terrain for waterfalls. Horizontal Catskill ledges and tilted Shawangunk formations are the raw material for many waterfall templates. Shawangunk waterfalls often generate on old fault lines. Where two types of rock come together, an area of differential erosion often develops and a stream will erode the softer rock faster. Over time, this differential rate of cutting can lead to a nearly vertical surface, and thus, a waterfall. Catskill waterfalls often form where a stronger layer of rock lies on top of a weaker one—this allows water to remove the lower layers while the resistant top layer creates a ledge for the water to leap.

Glaciers also played an important role in creating the region's waterfalls. During the ice age's four major advances, the entire area wore a thick blanket of ice. Up to a mile high, the ice bit deeply into the mountainous terrain, eroding, reshaping and polishing the bedrock. Valleys typically hosted the thickest parts of the ice sheets and lost more material to the glaciers' grinding action. In some places side valleys suffered less erosion and retain a higher topography. After the ice sheet retreated, the smaller valleys often had a large leap to make before merging with the wider valley downstream. Called a "hanging valley," these rugged, isolated terrains often inspire waterfalls. Many of the falls along the Catskills' eastern front form along the edge of hanging valleys.

The ice sheets also ripped into mountainsides forming new cliff faces and removing weaker rocks. Some of these differentially eroded surfaces also became waterfalls. Glacial till, the material dropped by melting glaciers, covers the entire region and many of its rock formations. The loose till often hides ledges, but once eroded, the newly exposed ledges form many of the region's smaller waterfalls. Many other streams had their valleys steepened and reworked by the ice, creating additional falls.

Waterfalls have a considerable impact on the surrounding environment. Within the stream course they cut off movement of fish and other aquatic animals. The upper or lower limit of a fish species in a stream is often determined by a waterfall (or in modern times a dam). Invasive species are kept from moving upstream, while the natural divisions isolate native populations. Trout are a good example of this situation. Introduced brown trout and rainbow trout cannot penetrate upstream once they hit a barrier such as a waterfall. Native brook trout populations are often protected from competition this way. On the other hand, areas that have lost brook trout populations cannot recover without assistance from people or nature's whim.

As the water launches into the air, it adds moisture and often cools the air temperature. Spray and moisture cover nearby rocks and slopes, creating distinct microenvironments. The area around a waterfall has more mosses, ferns, flowers and trees than surrounding areas. On most days it is easy to feel, as well as see the changes. A touch of cool perfumes the air. Everything is just a bit moister. Leaf litter is softer and darker, the moss a bit thicker and the understory more dense. Rocks are saturated with mosses that, in turn, are saturated with water. Everything is slippery. The forest immediately surrounding a New York waterfall is often a miniature rain forest.

Some waterfalls have spared the forest immediately surrounding their steep and isolated topography from man's enterprises. Nineteenth-century loggers were unable to profitably harvest trees in deep canyons, on precipitous cliffs, and along dangerous slopes. Some falls are in such difficult terrain that it was impractical to get men or equipment near them. It was too expensive and too dangerous. The very wilderness aspects people have come to appreciate today created the conditions that spared these forests from the bite of axe and saw. Of the few virgin hemlock groves remaining in the Catskills, Kaaterskill Falls, the Five Cascades and the many falls in Plattekill Clove account for three of these special places.

Even though waterfalls often appear as stalwart and timeless as the ridges and mountains nurturing them, a fall is not a stable landform. Over time, falls erode and quickly undermine the strength of the rock beneath them. Their steep slopes encourage erosion. Trees and boulders along a waterfall's margin tumble into the streambed from time to time. Some waterfalls migrate upstream as the water rips at the rocky foundation, while others decay into a slurry of cascades before merging with the rest of the watercourse. Some falls have their water pirated by a new channel or even a different stream. One season or a single event can have an impact on a fall's appearance or stability. Floods and high water move boulders and deposit trees near and below the falls. Geological change on a scale that humans can appreciate is a rule of thumb at a waterfall.

The Catskills' and Shawangunks' waterfalls have inspired artisans and outdoorsmen for generations. Painters from the Hudson River School of Art brought natural wonders such as Kaaterskill Falls, Haines Falls and Fawn's Leap to the culture of the western world. Thomas Cole's *Kaaterskill Falls*, Sanford Gifford's *Kaaterskill Clove* and Asher B. Durand's *Kindred Spirits* are all set among the region's waterfalls. Kaaterskill Falls in particular has been a long-time favorite, attracting generations of vacationers and local residents to its long ribbon of plunging water.

In a time before photography, paintings were one of the best ways people could communicate a sense of place. Attention to detail held a prestige that the camera would later replace. The best painters and their works were in great demand, and works of art by the new world's best artists were not affordable to the masses. People would line up in cities in America and Europe and pay a small fee to get a glimpse of the untamed American wilderness, which included places like Kaaterskill Falls and Plattekill Clove.

As technology brought photography into the mainstream,

stereoviews and postcards of these and many other Catskill and Shawangunk falls made them as popular as Niagara Falls, Half Dome and the Grand Canyon are today. Pictures of New York's waterfalls became household images. Evolving photographic techniques created new ways to see waterfalls, as long exposures created a cotton-candy look. At the same time, the Catskills' and Shawangunks' resort business boomed. In the mid- and late nineteenth century, high society, followed by the middle class, flocked to the mountains. People came to resorts such as the Catskill Mountain House, Hotel Kaaterskill, Laurel House and Mohonk Mountain House to escape summer's heat and see the area's many natural wonders, including its spectacular waterfalls.

Today, waterfalls are mainly the purview of those who visit and enjoy the natural world, but in the previous three centuries waterfalls were a driving engine of industry. What may seem to be timeless and pristine among New York's preserved lands was often a focal point for employment and manufacturing. Prized for their power rather than their beauty, falls were dammed and harvested to grind grain, saw timber, run smithies and, as technology advanced, provide electrical power. A few of the region's waterfalls, such as High Falls, remain enslaved for power generation while many others, such as Sheldon Falls, retain vestiges of their previous captivity.

Kaaterskill Falls is a curious blend of cultural admiration. It has been a special destination for more than a century and a half, but has not been immune from man's evolving relationship with the environment. The falls are spectacular, the highest in New York State, and have been a favored destination for generations. Today, the falls appear clothed in wilderness, free from buildings, roads and other signs of man's taming of the planet. The scene was much different in the 1800s. In 1852 the Laurel House opened atop the falls. No view of the falls was free of the hotel and its outbuildings. Long flights of wooden stairs lined the falls from top to bottom. Trains chugged along two sets of tracks nearby, their steam and wheels adding discord to the natural sound of falling water. Along the track routes, pieces of fallen coal remain fairly easy to find. In the surrounding areas, lumber companies stripped the mountains of their forests. Hemlock bark provided the needed acids for leather tanning, and Catskill waterfalls provided power for the tanneries.

Waterfalls are natural magnets for people, yet it is important that these places receive the care and stewardship they need to remain the beautiful retreats they have become. With so many people trying to enjoy so many places with so little capacity for dealing with human impact, only through awareness and conservation can waterfalls' beauty be ensured. Upon finding a favorite place or two, share your personal support for the area by joining local conservation groups, educating other people, setting a good example and trying to leave these places better than when you found them.

In this book Russell Dunn brings the best of the region's waterfalls to center stage, sharing each fall's unique characteristics in ways that will appeal to any waterfall admirer. In all, this book visits more than a half-mile of falling water from cute, babbling cascades to massive rock-crushing torrents. Every one of the waterfalls offers something unique and provides a new insight into the forces of Mother Nature, and oftentimes ourselves as well. In many ways waterfalls are like nature's dessert—an explosion of sweets for the eyes—and Dunn's recipes for enjoying them are truly a gourmet outdoor experience. Be prepared to be inspired!

Edward G. Henry
author of *Catskill Trails* (in two volumes) and *Gunks Trails*
13 July 2004

Introduction

Waterfalls by their very nature are chameleons, changing and altering shape according to the weather and seasons. During winter's deep freeze they are muted and immobile, indistinguishable from the still, motionless landscape around them. Coming upon an exceptionally high waterfall a hiker may occasionally hear the "thunk" of an ice ax as determined climbers struggle up a world that has gone vertical and frozen. Otherwise all remains silent except for the faint, gurgling sound of water running beneath the thick ice coat.

In spring, waterfalls abruptly turn into thunderous walls of writhing, cascading water, irresistible, chaotic, and unceasing. To stand in their way is to be swept into oblivion. Under the magical spell of spring, the frenetic activity of waterfalls is matched by the regeneration of life on land; skeletal trees burst into mosaics of deep green, the air fills with flying birds and insects, and the ground swells with scampering mammals.

Come summer, waterfalls gradually become sedate and languid, returning to life only periodically when thunderstorms release sudden, prodigious downpours of water. They are transformed by summer's desiccation into entities of rock, moss-covered, with rivulets streaming down their broad ledges. They invite contemplation and rest, and their quiet pools of cool water provide swimming holes for hikers seeking relief from the searing heat.

In autumn, waterfalls are framed by rainbows of color and become re-animated as surrounding streams and rivers fill again with water. Rippling water reflects the myriad of colors that fill the forest canopy. It is a time to watch leaves being swept endlessly over the falls and to try to predict exactly when and where they will reappear in the stream far below.

Regardless of season, waterfalls are fun to visit at any time of year. Although each waterfall may alter its complexion with the season, its essence remains unchanged, ultimately determined by the composition and shape of the underlying bedrock and the volume of water carried by the stream.

Sedimentary rocks such as shale and sandstone are eroded easily by the action of water in motion, creating carved and sculpted streambeds when conditions are just right. Metamorphic rocks, like slate and marble, often are more resistant to erosion and not as likely to be modified and sculpted by the stream. The third type—igneous rocks—are not likely to be found at the waterfalls described in this book.

Water flow volume, which creates the face of the waterfall, is determined not only by snow melt and rainfall; it is greatly affected also when the surrounding forest begins its production of new growth, which siphons away copious amounts of groundwater that would otherwise be released into the streams. For these reasons waterfalls typically languish during the summer.The personality of a waterfall is determined by its underlying bedrock and flow of water, but what ultimately determines its overall attractiveness? No right or wrong answer exists. Beauty is in the eye of the beholder. The presence of moss or shrubs, for instance, can lend pleasing notes of green to the waterfall during the summer, and bright reds and oranges during the fall. Some people enjoy conifers and the smell of fresh pine at waterfalls. They are enraptured by the ghostly whistle of wind through evergreens. Others delight in seeing deciduous trees with their densely packed leaves and changing foliage.

When waterfalls are formed in gorges, it's not unusual for an optical illusion to occur. A 60-foot-high waterfall in a medium-sized gorge can look positively mammoth, but when formed in a deeper, larger gorge with towering side walls, it is far less impressive. As Einstein pointed out, everything is relative.

Waterfalls are part of nature's destructive forces. Relentlessly they dismantle mountains, bringing down grains, pebbles, rocks, and boulders, one piece at a time. Paradoxically, they are also life-givers. Waterfalls churn up vast volumes of water, adding dissolved oxygen to the flow and in the process promoting life in the ecosystems of streams and lakes. When running at full throttle, waterfalls also produce tremendous updrafts of spray which settle over the surrounding land, promoting the growth of mosses, lichens, and plant life. A waterfall can turn the neighboring land into a living oasis even when the surrounding ground is brown and desiccated.

Why Do Waterfalls Exist?

Waterfalls are the products of an imperfect world. They are the end result of the cosmic, unifying forces of *imperfection* that drive all change and evolution. If Lamaitre's cosmic egg had been perfectly stable, for instance, then the "Big Bang," showering the universe with matter and energy, would never have occurred. If all matter had been perfectly distributed as the universe expanded, then planets and stars would not have coalesced, and there would be no Earth. If Earth were not an imperfectly shaped sphere, then there would be no upthrusted areas of land—only a planet-girdling ocean of unvarying depth.

If the weather were perfect, there would be no winds generated by a rotating Earth and its unevenly heated surface. Water would evaporate and then rain straight down again, never to be carried inland to the mountains and valleys so that rivers and streams might be created.

If Earth's bedrock were perfectly constituted, all rock would be of the same composition and erode at the same rate, producing long gullies and ravines to channel water down to the oceans, but not ledges and drops along the way to form waterfalls.

Waterfalls exist because of imperfection, a fact for which we should be eternally grateful. Were it not for the imperfect transmission of our own DNA from one generation to the next, there would be no evolution and, hence, no you nor I to marvel at the existence of waterfalls.

May this book, then, lead you to some of nature's most marvelous creations, the ultimate handiwork of an imperfect yet wondrous world. Herein are waterfalls that are tall and mighty, like Kaaterskill Falls and Awosting Falls, and waterfalls that are small and inviting, like Diamond Notch Falls and Split Rock Falls.

The book is divided into two sections: the Catskill Mountains and the Shawangunk Mountains. Although these regions are in close proximity, they differ significantly in terms of the rocks composing them and how the mountains were formed. This, in turn, leads to differences in the character of the waterfalls that each mountain range has produced. Waterfalls in the Catskills are the aftermath of an eroded plateau, and thus have been modified more drastically by their streams than have their Shawangunk cousins; Shawangunk waterfalls typically plunge over cliff faces whose rocks still actively resist the abrasive action of its streams.

The majority of the hikes in the upper, mountainous regions of the Catskills and the Gunks involve a trek of some distance in order to reach the waterfall. If you enjoy challenges and good exercise, then these are the hikes to undertake. In the lower elevations, however, more and more of the waterfalls described are roadside-accessible. Why is this? The answer has to do with the privatization of land. Below the mountainous regions, where the majority of state lands and parks can be found, the forests increasingly become parceled-off private land that is posted, blocking access to waterfalls. When waterfalls on private land are not visible from roadside, then for all practical purposes they are inaccessible. Where waterfalls are found next to a bridge or roadway, however, they remain in the public domain, as it were, and can be enjoyed from the roadside.

The inclusion of roadside waterfalls in this guide, then, is a necessity in order to include waterfalls in the valleys and lower regions of the Gunks and Catskills. But there is more to it than that. Roadside waterfalls are accessible to virtually everyone, including the elderly, the disabled, families with very young children, or those who simply have limited time or inclination for long treks. This book is meant as a guide for all people, of all levels of ability and motivation.

History of Waterfalls

Many of the waterfalls in this book were harnessed as tireless workhorses to power the factories and industries that were built on all of the major streams in this region starting in the mid-1600s when Europeans first entered what is now New York State, and continuing through the intervening centuries right up to the present. These waterfalls have turned waterwheels and driven turbines and generators to run cider presses, bellows, grinders, vertical saws and buzz saws, trip-hammers—virtually every kind of hand tool that formerly required human muscle. Until the advent of steam power, waterfalls provided the main source of energy that led to the industrial revolution and the westward expansion of our country.

Waterfalls have served as more than just beasts of burden, however. According to legend, Timothy Murphy, an eighteenth-century Indian fighter, avoided a pursuing war party by hiding behind a falling curtain of water at Bouck Falls on Panther Creek. Perhaps James Fenimore Cooper knew of this account, for in his classic story, *The Last of the Mohicans,* Hawkeye, Uncas, Chingachgook, Alice, Cora, and the rest of their small group take refuge at Coopers Cave at the base of Glens Falls to forestall capture by a Huron war party. The exploits of these heroes of fiction and folklore imitate the water ouzel (American dipper), a species of bird found in the western United States that builds its nests behind waterfalls in order to evade predators.

Waterfalls are favorites of daredevils. Annie Taylor was the first of a succession of daredevils to go over the 165-foot-high precipice of Niagara Falls in a barrel for fame and fortune (with little of either ever actually realized). What is most amazing about Annie Taylor's exploit is not that she did it at a time when it was unacceptable for women to engage in dangerous or outlandish activities, but that she was sixty-two years old on October 24, 1901, when she accomplished the feat. In the fall of 2003, a dubious waterfall record was set when Kirk Jones became the first human ever to survive a plunge over Niagara Falls without the benefit of a life jacket or other protective gear. Up to that point the only other person to survive the plunge (aside from the barrel riders) was Roger Woodward, a seven-year-old boy wearing a life jacket. Tightrope walkers (called funambulists) have crossed over the Niagara Gorge downstream from the falls, the most famous being Jean Francois Gravelet (a.k.a. Blondin) in the late 1850s.

In the Capital Region of New York State, Bobby Leach went over 65-foot-high Cohoes Falls in a barrel twice at the end of the nineteenth century. No doubt there are other stories of local derring-do as well.

Some cascades possessing flat, inclined surfaces have attracted local youths who ride down them as though on a waterslide. This is an activity that should be pursued very cautiously, if at all; once the ride begins, there is no turning back until the bottom is reached, and a lot of things can go wrong in between.

Waterfalls are nature's gift to weary hikers.

Keep in mind that all of the big waterfalls in New York State have histories of fatalities associated with them, generally from hikers getting too close to the top and being swept over the edge or slipping as they attempt to jump from high ledges.

More recently a new breed of daredevil has emerged. These are white-water kayakers who enjoy the thrill of launching themselves over the tops of waterfalls and riding them down. The current world record was established in 2003 when Ed Lucero plummeted 105.6 feet down Canada's Alexandra Falls. This activity is highly dangerous, of course, and those who pursue it accept the possibility that if things go wrong, they could be seriously injured or killed from the impact of hitting the water or sub-surface rocks, or drowned if they are caught in the rollers and not able to break free in time.

Fortunately, there is no need to perform any stunts or undertake any dares in order to enjoy the many waterfalls that you will be visiting in this book.

A Waterfall Illusion

In the field of optics there is a well-known, documented phenomenon called the "motion after-effect illusion." It's a fascinating optical illusion, and one that you can try the next time you are standing at a waterfall. Stare intently at the waterfall for twenty to thirty seconds and then look away, fixing your vision on a stationary object, such as a rock. The stationary object will seemingly move in a direction opposite from the water's motion. It's an interesting effect that reveals how the eye can be fooled into seeing motion when none is present.

The Grin Factor

Some waterfall enthusiasts contend that people who hike to waterfalls smile more and seem generally happier during the excursions than those who hike to other destinations. This belief is based upon an unproven hypothesis: waterfalls release negative ions (just as an electrical storm does) that stimulate the production of serotonin in the brain, which promotes a general feeling of well-being and happiness. You be the judge. But one thing is certain: everyone loves a waterfall!

Types of Waterfalls

There are numerous systems that have been devised for identifying and cataloging waterfalls. The categories we have selected are taken from Greg Parson & Kate B. Watson's recently released book, *New England Waterfalls*, and provide a common reference for differentiating one style of waterfall from another:

Block—a waterfall that is wider than its height, generally spanning the entire width of the stream. Such waterfalls are typically called "classic" or "horseshoe."

Cascade—a series of small drops and chutes, where the streambed is inclined.

Fan—a waterfall with a stream that starts off narrow at the top and widens as it makes its descent.

Horsetail—a nearly vertical drop of water, but with a stream that essentially stays in contact with the underlying bedrock.

Plunge—a vertical drop, usually from an overhanging ledge, straight down to the streambed below.

Punchbowl—a fall where the water is contracted into a narrow corridor and then ejected into a plunge pool.

The reality, of course, is that a waterfall may be a combination of one or more of these features, or have none of them at all. That's what makes each waterfall so unique and special; no two are ever alike.

Estimating a Waterfall's Height

Is there a way to accurately measure the height of a waterfall without dropping a plumb line over its crest? The answer is yes, and is to be found in high school trigonometry. You need a notebook, clinometer (for determining angles of inclination), and a range finder (for determining distance). The rest is mathematics. For those who are interested in learning more about determining a waterfall's height, we recommend "Ruth's Waterfalls of the Finger Lakes and Rochester, NY" on the website, www.naturalhighs.net. This website is the brainchild of Ruth Hopkins who, along with her husband, Roger, has explored many waterfalls in western New York and beyond. They even recently purchased a house with (what else?) a waterfall in the backyard.

Ruth's website points out that gravity also can be used for crudely estimating waterfall height. Simply throw a rock out horizontally from the top of a large waterfall (first making sure beyond doubt that no one is below), then use a stopwatch to time how long it takes the rock to hit the bottom of the gorge. Ruth provides the necessary tables for then calculating the waterfall's height.

Hunting for Waterfalls

If your interest in waterfalls grows beyond the scope of this book and you wish to make your own discoveries, buy a series of topographic (topo) maps covering the area that you plan to explore. Topo maps, read correctly, provide a three-dimensional view of the terrain as though looking down from an airplane, but without obscuring features like trees, bushes, clouds or fog. Streams and lakes on topo maps are represented by the color blue and will be named, if known. Note the blue lines of streams and rivers: these are where waterfalls will be indicated, if they exist.

Topo maps are particularly helpful for delineating changes in elevation and for showing the shapes of land masses. This is done through the use of contour lines. The more compressed the lines, the greater the change in elevation. In instances where tightly compressed contour lines cross the blue line of a stream, one may assume with a fair degree of confidence that a large waterfall may be found there. It is important to remember, however, that topo maps only show changes in elevation according to the map's overall level of detail. Large scale maps, for instance, may not show features less than 100 feet in size. A 70-foot waterfall, hence, would be invisible. On a smaller scale, more-detailed topo map, where features are revealed down to 25 feet in size, a 75-foot waterfall would be obvious. Using a regular, fairly detailed topo map, waterfalls down to a size of perhaps 20 feet in height may be spotted.

Is it possible to tell if there are waterfalls less than 20 feet in height on a particular stream? The answer is "maybe." A good topo map will afford some clues, but at some point one must rely upon intuition. For instance, if the contour lines on the map become compressed on both sides of a stream, it may be assumed that the river is passing through a gorge. As experience at map reading grows, intuition may suggest the possibility of a waterfall's being contained within the gorge or at the head of the ravine.

Waterfall hunting is a "hit or miss" venture, but it is the exploration and the uncertainty of knowing for sure what will be found at the end of the trail that adds excitement and a sense of adventure to what otherwise might be a predestined, run-of-the-mill hike.

Sometimes viable leads may be obtained by stopping in a small village or a town and just asking around. This method of waterfall discovery is also, of course, a "hit or miss" venture. Many times, residents who have lived in a town for all of their lives are completely unaware of a large waterfall that sits practically in their backyard. At other times someone may be found who ultimately proves to be a fountain of information. Teenagers are particularly helpful. Inevitably they know the places that their elders may have forgotten about or never actually visited.

Even though many waterfalls are on private land and posted, take heart. Sometimes only one side of the stream, typically along the bank containing the pathway, is off limits. A bushwhack along the non-posted side of the creek may afford a legal view of the waterfall and a perspective rarely seen by others. At other times landowners may be gracious enough to permit access across their land to a waterfall, particularly if they know the only purpose is to look and take pictures, and nothing more.

The waterfalls contained in this guidebook have been selected for all levels of ability. Some will involve a strenuous hike to get a view, while others can be seen easily from roadside.

While this book does not claim to be comprehensive, if every waterfall contained herein is visited, one will have seen the majority of significant waterfalls in the Catskills and Gunks that are accessible to the public.

Degree of Difficulty

The following terms are used to describe the difficulty levels of the hikes and excursions in this book:

Easy—less than 1.0 mile one way, with mostly even terrain and minimal elevation change.

Moderate—1.0 to 2.5 miles one way, with mixed terrain and some elevation change.

Difficult—more than 2.5 miles one way, with significant elevation change and mixed terrain, possibly including some rock scrambling.

Waterfall Preservation

Efforts continue today throughout the region to preserve major waterfalls and other natural wonders. For this, we are especially grateful to the State of New York, particularly the Department of Environmental Conservation (DEC), which has done much to keep the wilderness forever wild. We are also indebted to local land conservancies, the ADK (Adirondack Mountain Club), the AMC (Appalachian Mountain Club), the New York-New Jersey Trail Conference, the Open Space Institute, the Mohonk Preserve, and to all other groups and organizations that have worked tirelessly for wilderness preservation.

In all too many instances, natural scenic wonders like waterfalls and gorges have become permanently inaccessible as landowners built private homes nearby, closed off acres of surrounding land in order to enhance privacy, or grew leery of interlopers crossing their property who might then turn around and sue them if they became injured. I am idealistic and believe waterfalls are children of nature, born to be wild and as free as the streams they carry. Waterfalls should be open for all to enjoy and not be possessed and controlled by individuals with the power to do whatever they want with a natural wonder that nature has taken eons to create.

So much for idealism—now, back to reality:

Safety First

Before leaving home, make sure that safety is first on your list. Be proactive and anticipatory. Outdoor recreational activities are, by their very nature, potentially hazardous and contain certain risks. All participants in such activities must assume the responsibility for their own actions and safety. No book can replace good judgment. The outdoors is forever changing. The author and the publisher cannot be held responsible for inaccuracies, errors, or omissions, or for changes in the details of this publication, or for the consequences of any reliance on the information contained herein, or for the safety of people in the outdoors.

1. If you are hiking alone or in a small group, be sure to notify someone of your destination and expected time of arrival home. Make sure that person knows what action to take if you have not returned by the designated hour.

2. Only bushwhack through the woods if you are (1) an experienced hiker (2) know how to use a compass and have one with you (3) are prepared to spend several days in the woods if necessary (4) are with a group of similarly prepared hikers and (5) follow rule # 1.

3. Wear good hiking boots. Sneakers and shoes simply do not provide adequate support or traction, especially if you are scampering about on wet rocks and boulders, or negotiating steep inclines—conditions you are very likely to find at waterfalls and gorges.

4. Wear a long sleeved shirt and long pants to ward off pesky biting insects and the possibility of contracting Lyme disease or one of a variety of other insect-born ailments. Be sure to apply plenty of deet-based repellent on exposed skin for maximum protection, and wear appropriate sun protection to prevent harm to exposed skin.

5. Approach waterfalls, whenever possible, from the base. This will afford you the safest *and* best view, as you will be looking up at the cascade and taking in its full measure. Never walk out onto the top of a waterfall. Avoid any exposure where you could tumble from a height if you lose your footing. Never put yourself in the position where there is nothing to stop you from going over the edge if you start to slip.

6. Be extra careful climbing over or around rocks that are wet, moss-covered, or slippery. Rock surfaces can become slick when covered with water or slime. Don't take any chances when prudence and good judgment can make the difference between spending the summer hiking on the trail, or hobbling around on a pair of crutches.

7. Take along a hiking staff or collapsible pole to increase your

balance whenever traversing variable terrain such as rocky streambeds, or paths that are littered with roots and rocks.

8. Always maintain three points of contact if you are climbing up or down a steep ravine.

9. Dress according to the season. Be sure to take along extra layers of clothing in case the weather and temperature change dramatically. Avoid cotton clothes, which offer no insulation when wet.

10. Always carry survival gear such as an emergency medical kit, compass, flashlight, matches, whistle, high-energy food, an adequate supply of water (at least 24 ounces per person), and a small tarp. Do not drink untreated water. Giardia is not a pleasant memento to bring back from your hike.

11. Do not take shortcuts. They can lead to unanticipated hazards as well as subjecting the terrain to needless, additional erosion.

12. Heed trail markers and signs. Blowdown and other natural obstacles can cause trails to be rerouted. If posted signs appear where public access was presumed, respect the wishes of private landowners and go no further.

Many waterfalls have been harnessed to power waterwheels and turbines.

13. Always know where you are. Guidebooks, maps, and compasses are essential if you venture out into the wilderness. A GPS unit is also worth bringing along. Nothing, however, is a substitute for good judgment and basic common sense.

14. Never jump or dive off rocks or ledges into inviting pools of waters around waterfalls. Too many people have slipped and tumbled onto the rocks below, or have collided with unseen and unknown hazards below the water's surface.

15. Leave the area immediately if the weather is cool and you become accidentally soaked. Even 50° temperatures can produce hypothermia if you remain outside for too long after being immersed.

16. If you are standing at the base of a high waterfall, watch out for falling rocks—particularly those that may be inadvertently pitched off by an unthinking child or adult standing at the top.

17. Stay away from overhanging precipices of ice. People have died when blocks of ice have suddenly broken off from the rock face.

18. Watch out for hunters during deer season, even if you are on well-traveled trails.

19. Avoid cornering any wild animal at the bottom of a deep gorge as you approach a waterfall. If the animal has nowhere to retreat and feels threatened, it may seek a way out that goes right over you.

If you follow these common-sense recommendations, you are most likely to have a fun-filled, trouble-free hiking adventure. Just remember that nature is inherently wild and therefore unpredictable. Always be prepared for the unexpected.

And keep your ears attuned and your eyes wide open, for waterfalls will call to you!

W a t e r f a l l s

falling

in endless repetition
the past echoes through the sounds of water,
spilling timeless,
character born of rocky design
hidden and powerful

mesmerizing

droplets of mist
crown foam-covered flutes
rushing in cascades,
a constancy of motion
inextricable and beautiful

connecting

a juncture between
reflective streams above and
turbulent waters below,
freefall transition unifying
creation and source

descending

over and over
stone precipice worn
smooth with persistence,
nature's essence revealed
deep and true

remembering

eons stand witness
to what mortals cannot see
and fear to contemplate,
eternity turning
slowly and assured

calling

to time, flowing
with life, creating new
moments in perpetual chain,
traveling toward the end
elemental and shared.

©jZoske, 14 April, 2002

Section I

The Catskills form the northern terminus of the Allegheny Plateau—a great raised area of land that extends all the way south to Tennessee. Because their rocks have endured the erosive effects of wind, rain, snow, ice, and life itself comparatively well, the Catskills are generally 2000 feet higher than other sections of this expansive plateau.

To be sure, the Catskills are not your typical mountain range. Unlike the Shawangunks to the south, the Catskills were raised up as one flat, solid piece. As a result, the beds of rock that underlie the mountains are horizontal, and not folded as they would be if the land was buckled.

At one time the Catskill plateau was several thousand feet higher than it is today. The fact that it no longer looks like a plateau, but rather a mountainous region, is because of the many streams and rivers that have dissected it and created the valleys and notches that can be seen today.

The rocks forming the Catskills are sedimentary, such as sandstone, red shale, and conglomerates (the so-called "puddingstones" that can be seen along the escarpment trail leading northward from the site of the old Catskill Mountain House). What's interesting is that the Catskills are a one-sided range of mountains, presenting a 2000-foot vertical face to the east, called the "Wall of Manitou," and then gradually merging into the Allegheny Plateau to the west without any clear-cut line of demarcation. The reason for this is that the bedrock of the eastern Catskills is much coarser, and therefore more naturally resistant to erosion. Furthermore, the porosity of its rocks tends to minimize the ability of streams to gather enough water to wear them down. As a result, the eastern Catskills are noticeably higher than the western Catskills, which are primarily composed of weaker sandstones and shales.

Not surprisingly, then, the highest waterfalls in the Catskills, such as Kaaterskill Falls, Haines Falls, and the multiple falls in Platte Clove, tend to be on the eastern side where the rocks are tougher and the elevation higher.

Waterfalls of the Catskills

Geologists believe that the eastern edge of the Catskills once extended as much as two miles further into the Hudson Valley. The fact that all this rock was ultimately evacuated by the Hudson River is probably what gives the eastern rampart of the Catskills such a clearly defined edge.

Although the Catskills contain surprisingly few lakes and ponds in comparison with the Adirondacks, they do possess their own unique bodies of water—the reservoirs. These are, in descending order of size, the Ashokan, Pepacton, Cannonville, Rondout, Neversink, and Schoharie (Gilboa) reservoirs. The reservoirs do little to serve the needs of local residents, however. The water collected is transported south through large underground aqueducts to downstate residents, especially in New York City.

The reservoirs have had a small, but significant impact on Catskills waterfalls. Devasego Falls, for instance, was lost forever when the town of Gilboa was inundated so that the Schoharie Reservoir could be created. Several waterfalls also have lost some of their power and luster because large amounts of water have been siphoned off from their streams by a reservoir.

Past glacial epochs have had a decided impact on waterfall formation. According to *Glacial Geology of the Catskills:* "Throughout the Catskills, many small waterfalls and cascades occur where tributary streams have been shifted to one side, as they enter the main valleys, by deposits of thick drift plastered across the mouths of their valleys."[1]

The writings of Washington Irving and John Burroughs, along with the paintings of Thomas Cole, Frederic Church, and other landscape artists from the Hudson River School, served to fire the imaginations of early Victorians, who thronged to the Catskills and its beautiful gorges and waterfalls to find excitement and exhilaration.

One legend has it that the Native American name for the Catskills was *Onteora,* or "Land in the Sky," which is fitting for a place where waterfalls seemingly tumble down from the heavens.

742:—KAATERSKILL FALLS.
HAINES FALLS. CATSKILL MTS. N.Y.

At 231 feet there is no waterfall higher than Kaaterskill Falls in the Catskills.

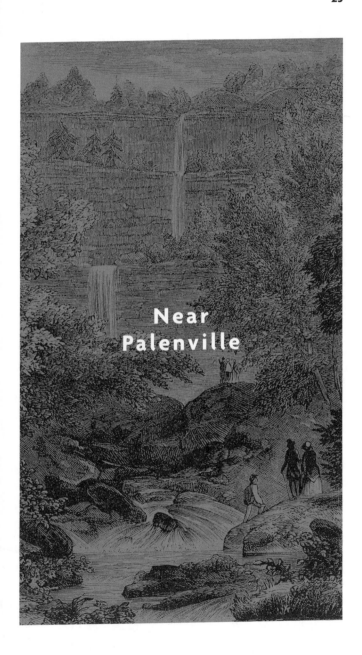

Near
Palenville

Falls in Sleepy Hollow Notch

Location: North of Palenville (Greene County)

Accessibility: 0.2-mile hike round-trip along an old carriage road that ascends steadily uphill; 2.0-mile hike round-trip if you wish to reach the site of the Rip Van Winkle House at the top of the notch.

Degree of Difficulty: Easy, with an initial steep ascent; Moderate to site of the Rip Van Winkle House

Description: There are a number of small to medium-sized cascades formed on Stony Brook, a small stream that rises on the eastern shoulder of North Mountain and flows through Sleepy Hollow, entering Kaaterskill Creek just slightly southwest of the intersection of Rtes. 23A & 32. Stony Brook also has been called Rip Van Winkle Brook and Sleepy Hollow Brook in times past.

Roland Van Zandt, writing about Sleepy Hollow in *The Catskill Mountain House*, states, "As anyone may discover who visits the 'wild ravine' today, the innumerable pools, glens and falls that border the first mile of the steep ascent are as refreshing and beautiful as they were during the hottest summers of the nineteenth century."[1]

Three pretty cascades, consisting of consecutive drops of 12 feet, 5 feet, and 4 feet, can be seen from the bank of the stream next to the carriage road near the beginning of the hike. There are additional cascades and falls as you hike up through the notch, but they become increasingly harder to see as the carriageway pulls away from the streambed. Through most of the hike, the old carriage road follows an easement through private lands, which are noticeably posted on both sides of the road.

Shortly after you cross over Black Snake Bridge—a small wooden bridge that spans a tiny tributary to Stony Brook—the land to the right is state land and you are free to explore the upper regions of the clove. Unfortunately, the land to your left, where the ravine and upper cascades are, remains posted. From this point on, the stream becomes less energetic, and only minor cascades can be seen and heard far below. If you continue for another 0.3-0.4 mile, you will reach a point where the carriage road dramatically curves to the left at the head of the ravine. You have reached the top of Sleepy Hollow and the site where the Rip Van Winkle House once stood.

History: Sleepy Hollow, also known as Rip Van Winkle Hollow, is named after Washington Irving's famous fictitious character from a story of the same name published in 1819. Virtually all school-age children know the tale of how Rip Van Winkle, who escaped from his nagging wife for the afternoon and headed up into the mountains only to run into a motley crew of celebratory dwarves from Hendrick Hudson's crew. Joining in their revelry, Rip drank his fill of spirits and fell into a deep slumber. The slumber lasted twenty years, leaving Rip, when he awoke to return to the valley, a much older, enfeebled man. On the plus side, Rip no longer had a nagging wife to contend with.

According to legend, the hike up Stony Brook follows Rip's mythical route into the mountains. In the old days, Charles Beach's stagecoaches would make the climb up through the hollow, stopping midway at the Rip Van Winkle House before negotiating a wide turn and continuing up to the Pine Orchard, where the Catskill Mountain House waited.

The glen is described, fictitiously of course, by Irving: "On the other side he looked down into a deep mountain glen, wild, lonely and shagged, the bottom filled with fragments from the impending cliffs, and scarcely lighted by the reflected rays of the setting sun."[2]

Rockwell, in *The Catskill Mountains and the Region Around*, describes the entrance to Sleepy Hollow as follows: "Just south of the toll-gate, in the rear of the large farm-house, there is a saw-mill, on a small mountain stream, which comes rapidly down through a wild, deep, rocky ravine."[3]

Sleepy Hollow Notch was the most popular route to the Catskill Mountain House until 1882, when an elevating railroad was constructed nearby, making the carriage road virtually obsolete.

When you reach the point where the carriage road veers abruptly to the left at the head of the ravine, you will see old foundations—remnants of the Rip Van Winkle House that was built in 1845. Supposedly the hotel had a long bar to accommodate thirsty visitors. Near the foundations is Rip's Rock, a large, flat-sided rock where Rip miraculously fell asleep for 20 years.

The carriage road leading up through Sleepy Hollow is still quite impressive, although eroded in spots. Not only are there waterfalls in a deep ravine to your left, but towering cliffs and rocky spires above you to the right.[4]

Directions: From the village of Catskill, take Rt. 23A southwest to Palenville. When you arrive in Palenville, continue on Rt. 23A past the intersection of Rtes. 32A & 23A for less than 0.2 mile, then turn right onto Bogart Road, proceeding north. At 2.2 miles you will notice a parking area for visitors who are interested in using the horse trail. At 2.4 miles a road comes into Bogart Road from the right. When you reach 2.6 miles, turn left onto Mountain House Road. You will see a New York State sign indicating the way to the "Sleepy Hollow Horse Trail." Proceed uphill, driving west, for 0.7 mile until you come to the end of the road, which is near the site of the former Saxe's Farm Tollgate. Observe the "no parking" signs and park off to the side of the road just down from the road's terminus, beyond the old barn. You will see instructions, posted on the gate at the end of the road, on exactly how to proceed.

After parking, continue on foot to the gate at the end of the road

Saxe's Farm was once the gateway to Sleepy Hollow.

and follow the old carriage road (now a designated horse trail) west, which will take you through Sleepy Hollow. The falls begin within less than 0.1 mile from the gate, at the point where Stony Brook and the old carriage road parallel each other. All of the main falls can be found just before a posted secondary road goes off to the left. Just 40 feet further upstream, at the point where posted signs prohibit following a side road left and down to the stream and to a washed out bridge, a stunning 12-foot cascade drops into a semi-circular glen.

You can glimpse a couple of small cascades just upstream from this intersection, but from this point on the carriage road rises too high above the ravine for other falls to be observed easily, even when the leaves have fallen.

For equestrians, this is one "hike" you can take on horseback.

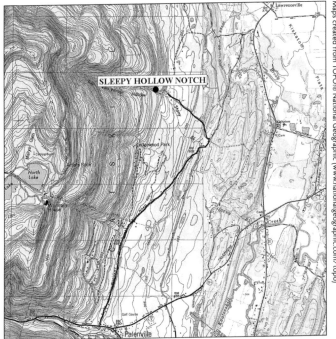

Fall on Lucas Kill

Location: Near Palenville (Greene County)

Accessibility: Roadside

Description: This small waterfall is formed on the Lucas Kill, a tiny stream that rises on the southeast shoulder of Kaaterskill High Peak and flows into the Plattekill north of the Saugerties Reservoir.

The waterfall is over 8 feet high and located on private land, but can be seen easily from roadside.

Directions: From Palenville, turn off of Malden Ave. (a road that parallels the south bank of Kaaterskill Creek) onto Woodstock Road and proceed south. The road quickly turns into Manorville Road. After roughly 2 miles you will come to an old stone bridge and the intersection with Ralph Vedder Road, on your left. The fall is directly to your right, visible from roadside.

From West Saugerties, just west of the bridge spanning the Plattekill Creek on Plattekill Road, turn onto Manorville Road and drive west for approximately 2 miles. The fall will be on your left as you cross over an old stone bridge.

If you are interested in viewing another small fall while in the vicinity, turn onto Ralph Vedder Road and drive east for 0.1 mile. A 4-foot waterfall, by roadside, will be to your right.

Cloves
of the
Catskills

The Catskills contain three principal cloves that have been used by travelers since the earliest days to make their way through the mountains—Kaaterskill Clove and Plattekill Clove oriented in an east-west direction, and Stony Clove, which runs north-south. The word "clove" comes from the Dutch word *kloof*, meaning a "ravine, hollow, or notch in the wall of a mountain or ridge." "Mountain pass" would be a fair synonym as well.

Kaaterskill Clove

Over the eons Kaaterskill Clove has been carved out and shaped by Kaaterskill Creek, a medium-sized stream that rises in the hills west of North Mountain and flows into Catskill Creek at Cauterskill, just west of the village of Catskill. *Kill* is the Dutch word for creek, making Kaaterskill Creek somewhat of a redundancy. Geologists estimate that Kaaterskill Clove was formed as far back as one million years ago during the Illinoisian Ice Age. The clove has gone through significant changes since then as subsequent ice ages modified its architecture.

According to geologist Robert Titus, a stupendous waterfall once existed in the clove, and was formed on a now-minuscule tributary that was fed by a retreating glacier high on top of North Lake. Titus estimates the cascade totaled 1,700 feet in height! "The entire course was very steep," writes Titus, "but the last 100 feet or so would have actually been a nearly vertical waterfall. This was probably a world-class drop of water ... beginning at about 2400 feet of elevation ... [to its] ... final crash at the very bottom of Kaaterskill Clove, there at an elevation of a mere 700 feet."[1]

J. Van Vechten Vedder, in *History of Greene County, New York, 1651-1800,* states that "we know but little of the Kaaterskill Clove before the advent of the tanneries, which was a later epoch in its history, but a pioneer geologist writes of numerous copperheads and rattlesnakes, eagles soaring overhead, of trees interlacing over the stream where five pound trout were caught; of perpendicular ledges covered by enormous rocks, over which waved the pine with its funereal verdure, often projecting over the cliffs like nodding plumes."[2] In *The Catskill Mountain House,* Roland Van Zandt describes the walls of the clove as looming "over the village of Palenville like towers and battlements of cyclopean structure."[3]

The clove has been transformed since these early days, principally by the introduction of Rt. 23A, known as the "Rip Van Winkle Trail," which has made the interior accessible to anyone with a motor vehicle.

Directions: Get off at Exit 21 of the NYS Thruway and proceed southwest, either by taking Rt. 23A out of Catskill until you reach the junction of Rtes. 23A & 32, or by going west on Rt. 23 and then proceeding south on Rt. 32 until you reach the junction of Rtes. 23A & 32.

From the junction of Rtes. 23A & 32, go west on Rt. 23A for 2.3 miles. When you reach the stoplight at the junction of Rtes. 32A & 23A you have arrived in the village of Palenville.

Palenville

Palenville, a small town that has been known in days past as "the village of falling waters" because of its many waterfalls, is the entry point to Kaaterskill Clove.

Palenville's history goes back to the mid-1700s when it served as a fortification during the Revolutionary War.

Following the War of 1812, Americans became free to engage in world trade without British interference. As a result, New York's tanning industry began its rapid expansion, fueled by the immense forests of hemlock that covered the Catskills. In 1817, Gilbert Palen built a tannery near the entrance to Kaaterskill Clove, and by so doing gave the town its name. Within several years other business followed, and Palenville became a thriving, rough-and-tumble tannery town.

By 1866, however—within the span of just half a century—every factory had closed. The tanning industry was dependent on vast quantities of hemlock trees (to tan just one hide required 13 cubic feet of bark), and when the great forests of the Catskills lay in ruins from the effects of deforestation, the tanning industry collapsed.

Fortunately, nineteenth-century civilization was developing a newfound appreciation for nature at the same time as the Catskill forests were being laid to waste. Cities were generally unpleasant places in which to live, with their industrial pollution, overcrowding, pestilences, and poor sanitation. The Catskill Mountains, with its abundance of waterfalls and stupendous gorges, became a Mecca for downstate residents and other tourists who wanted to escape from the city for a pleasant and invigorating stay in the country.

Palenville was able to capitalize on the rapidly expanding tourist industry by proclaiming itself to be the home of Washington Irving's fictional character Rip Van Winkle.

Along with the vacationers came many artists who were attracted by the wild natural beauty of the Catskills, especially the scenic wonders and waterfalls of Kaaterskill Clove. Collectively these nineteenth-century landscape painters and draftsmen became known as the Hudson River School, America's first homegrown artistic movement. And the village of Palenville, ideally situated at the entrance to Kaaterskill Clove, offered inexpensive boardinghouses that suited the small budgets of many of these artists, and has been credited as being America's first artist colony.

Falls at Tannery Bridge.

Roadside Tour:
Historic Waterfalls of Palenville

There are a number of waterfalls within the village of Palenville, all formed on Kaaterskill Creek. Unfortunately, most of these falls can be glimpsed only from afar and cannot be accessed directly because private homes have been built along both sides of the stream. Villagers have grown weary of trespassers trying to sneak through their backyards to glimpse the waterfalls. As a result, "no parking," "posted," and "keep out" signs abound throughout the residential section of the village. You can still get a partial look at these falls without trespassing, however, from the several roads that parallel the stream. By taking the following tour, either on foot or by car, you will be able to glimpse a number of the historic waterfalls that gave Palenville its nickname, "Village of Falling Waters." Just be sure to remain at roadside.

The tour begins at the junction of Rtes. 23A & 32A in the village of Palenville. If you are walking, park at a convenient spot along Rt. 23A.

From the junction of Rtes. 23A & 32A, turn onto Rt. 32A, going southeast for 0.1 mile. Turn right onto Woodstock Ave. At 0.1 mile you will cross over Kaaterskill Creek, where several pretty, 2-foot-high ledge falls can be seen from Tannery Bridge. The name of the bridge is a tribute to the origins of the village.

Continue straight ahead. At 0.2 mile from Woodstock Ave. turn right onto Mill Road. You will now be proceeding west along the south bank of Kaaterskill Creek. You will glimpse off to your right a 5-foot-high waterfall just past a small red barn. Look carefully as you continue past the fall and you will also observe an old footbridge that spans the creek just upstream from the falls.

After 0.3 mile turn right onto Malden Avenue and continue west, heading towards the section of stream that contains Ferndale Falls and Niobe Falls. You will see a 5-foot-high cascade in the stream where an old road once led down to the base of the cascade. At 0.4 mile the road comes to an end at a turnaround. From here a wide, block-shaped falls, diagonally angled in the streambed, can be seen by looking through the barbed wire fence at the end of a long wooden barrier that was created to give the homeowner some privacy and keep interlopers from accessing the gorge.

In times past, Malden Road continued out to Rt. 23A, but it was barricaded years ago when the bridge over Kaaterskill Creek needed to be replaced. Residents asked that the bridge not be replaced in order to reduce unnecessary traffic through the residential section of the village and to deter curiosity-seekers. Parking is prohibited at both ends of the barricaded section of Malden Road, which means there is little traffic, even on foot.

Another waterfall tour is available as you drive or walk along Rt. 23A through the semi-commercialized section of the village. Go west on Rt. 23A from the junction of Rtes. 23A & 32A, and in just over 0.4 mile you will pass by a waterfall visible off in the woods to your left. At 0.9 mile you will reach a bridge spanning Kaaterskill Creek at the western terminus of Palenville. If you look downstream carefully, you may be able to make out the distant brink of a fall. Unfortunately, this is the only view you can get of this fall because the land on both sides of the creek is posted—including the rock walls of Kaaterskill Creek itself!

A third walk or drive from the junction of Rtes. 23A & 32A will take you to Helena Falls. Proceed southeast on Rt. 32A for 0.4 mile until you reach a small bridge spanning Kaaterskill Creek. Park off to the side of the road. Looking below the bridge, you can see the top of the Helena Falls, which is 6-8 feet high. Looking upstream, a series of small ledge falls also can be seen. The appropriately named Waterfall Motel is located next to the falls.[1]

Helena Falls, another one of Palenville's roadside waterfalls.

Palenville Overlook

There are spectacular views from Palenville Overlook, a high promontory overlooking Palenville and Kaaterskill Creek. From this rocky bluff you can gaze nearly straight down into the village to observe many of the waterfalls that would otherwise be partially concealed behind houses and trees. Be sure to bring along binoculars and to undertake the hike in the early spring or late fall when the trees are bereft of leaves. You also can look upstream into Kaaterskill Clove itself and see the more distant falls at Moore's Bridge. Motorists driving back and forth through the clove cross over this bridge and never realize just how close they are to a beautiful little waterfall. The only disadvantage to viewing waterfalls from Palenville Overlook is that the distance and height tends to flat-

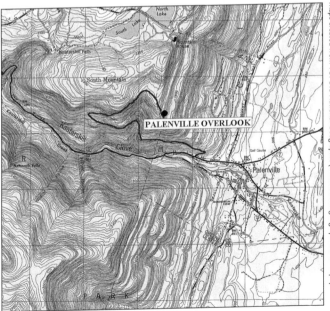

Maps created from TOPO!© National Geographic (www.nationalgeographic.com/topo)

ten out the falls, giving them a two-dimensional look and making them appear more like rapids than cascades.

To reach Palenville Overlook, take Rt. 23A west for 0.6 mile from the junction of Rtes. 23A & 32A in Palenville. Pull into a tiny parking area on your right that is 0.3 mile west of White's Road, just before the "Entering Catskill Park" sign.

Hike an old carriage road uphill for 2.5 miles, passing by such scenic sights as the Kaaterskill Clove Overlook and The Gulf. At one time this road, known as the Harding Road Trail after George W. Harding, owner of the Hotel Kaaterskill, led to the renowned hotel perched at the top of South Mountain. At 2.5 miles turn right onto the Sleepy Hollow Horse Trail. The trail gradually descends for 0.5 mile, going essentially east, until you reach the Palenville Overlook Junction. Turn right onto the yellow-blazed spur trail and walk south for 0.3 mile across level ground to the overlook.

Waterfalls in Lower Kaaterskill Clove

There are several historically significant waterfalls contained in Kaaterskill Clove between where the Rt. 23A bridge first crosses Kaaterskill Creek at the western terminus of Palenville, and its confluence with Lake Creek near the horseshoe turn by Bastion Falls. Of these, two are on public lands and one, Labelle Falls, is on private property. Unfortunately, the two on public lands—Moore's Bridge Falls and Fawn's Leap—are difficult to access because of a lack of parking areas.

Early photographs reveal a number of buildings and factories at the entrance to Kaaterskill Clove, just past the bridge spanning Kaaterskill Creek at the western edge of town. Looking at the entrance to the clove today, it is difficult to imagine that thriving scene.[1]

The current road going through Kaaterskill Clove is a far cry from its predecessor, which was made of packed dirt. A toll collector ensured that no one got through without payment. The tollgate usually was located near the bottom of the clove, but was at one time placed as far up the road as Fawn's Leap.[2]

Moore's Bridge Falls and Fawn's Leap

Moore's Bridge Falls

This pretty, 10-foot-high cascade is located directly under Moore's Bridge where Rt. 23A crosses over Kaaterskill Creek a second time, approximately 1.9 miles from the junction of Rtes. 23A & 32A in Palenville. What gives the waterfall its pleasing aspect is the reddish coloration that is contained in both the bedrock of the fall and in the walls of the ravine. The red coloration is the result of the area having once been part of the great Catskill Delta. When the sea level fell, the rock bed slowly reddened from oxidation.

There is no easy way to access this waterfall, since there are no roadside pull-offs next to the bridge. You may park in one of several tiny pull-offs approximately 0.1 mile east of the bridge; then walk west along the side of the road along the guardrail until you reach the bridge. Unless you are willing to stay off the road and out of traffic, however, this fall should be considered inaccessible.[1-3]

Fawn's Leap

Fawn's Leap is a 20-foot-high waterfall contained in a small chasm where Kaaterskill Creek collects itself before careening past Profile Rock and under Moore's Bridge. It is an area characterized by turbulent, rushing waters. Wildcat Ravine joins Kaaterskill Creek directly above the falls, and Hillyer Ravine enters just below. Although it is close to the roadside, Fawn's Leap remains hidden from view because of the way the streambed parallels the road at this point.[1-2]

According to legend, Fawn's Leap acquired its name from an incident involving a doe and fawn who were being pursued by a pack of dogs. The doe reached the gorge and was able to leap safely across its width to the other side. The fawn, however, lacked its mother's strength to vault the distance and fell into the stream, only to be swept over the top of the fall to its doom. Fawn's Leap has been known as Dog Hole and Dog Pool in past years, probably for the same reasons as it has been called Fawn's Leap. (It is not the Dog Hole pictured in R. Lionel De Lisser's book, *Picturesque Catskills: Greene County,* however.)[3]

In Rev. Charles Rockwell's book, *The Catskill Mountains and the Region Around,* written in 1867, the fall is described with such marvelous hyperbole that only a five-fold reduction in size during the last century could explain its current dimensions. According to Rockwell, "It lies in a narrow ravine, below the rocks where the Cauterskill comes down and falls over the shelf into a basin, an hundred feet lower down. The whole is surrounded and overhung by trees and shrubs common to the region, and forms an amphitheater of wildness and beauty seldom surpassed. It is not so capacious as

Fawn's Leap—one of the Catskills' most photogenic waterfalls. In the 19th century this was a favorite with Hudson River School painters.

the falls near Pine Orchard [Kaaterskill Falls] but has points of interest which surpass even that famous spot."[4]

With the exception of Kaaterskill Falls, and possibly Haines Falls, Fawn's Leap was the most popularized Catskill waterfall in early-twentieth-century postcards, and a favorite subject of painters of the nineteenth-century Hudson River School.

The fall, which has been privately owned in the past, was just recently acquired by the State of New York and is again open to the public. The problem, unfortunately, just as for the falls at Moore's Bridge, is accessing the fall.

Once again the only option is to park in one of several pull-offs east of Moore's Bridge and carefully make your way up to Moore's Bridge, staying on the side by the guardrail and away from traffic. From the bridge, the best approach to the base of the fall is to follow Kaaterskill Creek upstream for 0.05 mile, which is not as simple as it sounds; this short hike requires scrambling over ledges, around boulders, over fallen trees, and rock-hopping along the stream.

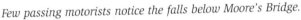

Few passing motorists notice the falls below Moore's Bridge.

Along the South Rim of Kaaterskill Clove: Viola Falls, Wildcat Falls, Buttermilk Falls and Santa Cruz Falls

Accessibility: Significant hike: 9.0 miles round-trip from Palenville; 12 + miles round-trip from Platte Clove

Degree of Difficulty: Difficult

Description: All four of these untamed waterfalls are formed at high elevations: Viola Falls at 1,400 feet; Wildcat Falls at 1,800 feet; Buttermilk Falls at 2,000 feet; and Santa Cruz Falls at over 2,000 feet. Santa Cruz Falls, in Santa Cruz Ravine, is by far the most famous of the four, but it is located on land privately owned by Twilight Park and is therefore not accessible to the public.

Viola Falls is formed in Hillyer Ravine on a tiny creek that rises on the east shoulder of Kaaterskill High Peak. The stream flows into Kaaterskill Creek between Moore's Bridge and Fawn's Leap. This waterfall, recessed and concealed, is not readily visible in its entirety from Rt. 23A below. The falls were named after the vast number of violets that can be found in close proximity to the falls. There are excellent views of Kaaterskill Clove from Poet's Ledge, slightly east of Hillyer Ravine.

Wildcat Falls is formed in Wildcat Ravine on a tiny stream that rises on the northeast shoulder of Kaaterskill High Peak and flows into Kaaterskill Creek near Fawn's Leap. Wildcat Falls has a tiny flow of water and is not easily seen from Rt. 23A. On the other hand, there are excellent views of the clove and the Hudson Valley from the top of the waterfall. The ADK *Guide to Catskill Trails: Catskill Region* describes the falls aptly: "This is a spectacular place. The stream drops precipitously from the great rock ledge. The view looks across the distant Hudson River directly at artist Frederic Church's home, Olana.[1] One feels a part of one of his Catskill paintings in this setting." (Olana is northeast of the village of Catskill, on hills overlooking the Hudson River and Rogers Island.)

Buttermilk Falls is formed on John Case Brook, a small stream that rises on the north slopes of Kaaterskill High Peak and flows into Kaaterskill Creek about halfway between Moore's Bridge and the horseshoe turn by Bastion Falls. According to Lee McAllister, in *Hiking the Catskills,* there is a "drop of 100 feet off the top of the falls."[2] In *The Catskill Mountain House,* Roland Van Zandt describes how the falls look when seen from below on Rt. 23A: "high on the southern rim of the clove one can see the cascading foam of Buttermilk Falls, at least a thousand feet above the surface of the road."[3] The ADK *Guide to Catskill Trails: Catskill Region* states that from Buttermilk Falls, "one can look almost down 2,000 feet below to the Rip Van Winkle Trail."[4]

Buttermilk Falls is not one continuous waterfall, but rather consists of three main cascades with a smaller, fourth drop of 15 feet.

Near the end of John Case Brook, at its confluence with Kaaterskill Creek, is an absolutely gorgeous waterfall that faces a number of old ruins along the north bank of Kaaterskill Creek. The ruins, known as East Hunter, date back to when Palenville and environs were a thriving tannery community.

Santa Cruz Falls is formed on a small stream that rises on the northeast shoulder of Roundtop Mountain and flows down through Santa Cruz Ravine into Kaaterskill Creek, just east of Kaaterskill Creek's confluence with Lake Creek. The falls are located on private lands and therefore are not accessible to the public. Santa Cruz Falls, however, can be easily seen and enjoyed from Rt. 23A, just east of the horseshoe turn at Bastion Falls. With a good pair of binoculars, you won't be disappointed, even though the view is a distant one.[5]

Viola, Wildcat, Buttermilk, and Santa Cruz Falls are impressive cataracts due to their elevations, but generally put on a show only during the early spring or following a heavy downpour. This is because the waterfalls have formed where there is a limited watershed.

History: The area adjacent Roundtop Mountain, along the top of Kaaterskill Clove and west of Kaaterskill High Peak, once contained a small Revolutionary War fort on its summit, where British-backed Tories and Indian allies kept vigilant watch over the valley below.

There are still bits of the foundation and earthenware visible.

Directions: There are several ways to access the high elevation waterfalls along the southern rim of Kaaterskill Clove:

Palenville Approach: It is imperative that you park in the commercial section of Palenville along Rt. 23A, or at the trailhead parking for the Palenville Overlook. There is no parking along Malden Lane, which houses private residences.

Walk south from the junction of Rtes. 32 & 23A, and turn right onto Woodstock Ave, which immediately crosses Kaaterskill Creek. Once you are on the other side of the stream, go straight past a left-

The southern wall of Kaaterskill Clove contains a series of towering waterfalls.

hand turn and then right onto Mill Road, which follows the stream west. This road soon veers to the left and comes out onto Malden Lane. Proceed right on Malden Lane and walk west for about 0.2 mile. On the left-hand side, between two houses, there are turquoise trail markers at the beginning of an old dirt road going uphill.

If you have parked at the trailhead for the Palenville Overlook, walk west along the side of Rt. 23A for 0.3 mile. As soon as you cross over the bridge spanning Kaaterskill Creek, go left. There is a barricade across the end of what used to be the terminus of Malden Lane. Walk around it and proceed east along this section of road that has been closed to traffic. You will soon come to a second barricade. Walk around it and continue on what is now Malden Lane. In less than 0.2 mile you will see the turquoise trail markers between two houses to your right, indicating the start of the trail.

From this point you will be hiking along a section of the famous Long Path, which extends all the way from the Helderbergs down to the George Washington Bridge in New York City. This road-like part of the trail was used to transport bluestone in the 1800s.

After hiking uphill and along the rim of Kaaterskill Clove for approximately 2.5 miles, you will reach a small stream leading down through a ravine. Follow this creek downstream for about 0.5 mile and you will reach Viola Falls, right at the junction of two small streams.

Hike back up to the main trail, and then continue westward for another 0.6 mile. Once again a stream will pass under the main trail. Follow this creek downstream for 0.1 mile and you will be at the top of Wildcat Falls.

Return to the main trail and continue west for 0.5 mile. This trek will lead you to Buttermilk Falls, which is virtually on the main trail.

Altogether, be prepared for a substantial hike of 9.0 miles round-trip (including side trips) from the trailhead.

Platte Clove Approach: An alternate way of accessing the falls is to hike in from the top of Platte Clove, which is a large canyon to the south of Kaaterskill Clove. The hike from Platte Clove involves a longer trek, but one with a less vigorous ascent since it starts at a high elevation to begin with.

From West Saugerties, drive up Platte Clove Mountain Road (a seasonal road) to the top of the clove. Park in an area on the left just before crossing over an old stone bridge where a very deep and treacherous ravine can be found.

From the parking area walk west along Platte Clove Mountain Road, and then follow the blue-blazed markers for the Long Trail, which follows a snowmobile trail uphill in a northward direction. During the next 3 miles you will be skirting around Kaaterskill High Peak (elevation 3,655 feet), which until the 1870s was thought to be the highest peak in the Catskill Mountains. (It isn't; Slide Mountain is, at an elevation of 4,180 feet.)

After hiking for 3.5 miles, you will reach a junction. The snowmobile trail continues to your left and the blue-blazed trail proceeds straight, descending quickly. Continue straight on the blue-blazed trail. From this point it is roughly 1.5 miles further to Buttermilk Falls, 2.0 miles to Wildcat Falls, and 2.6 miles to Viola Falls, traversing what was at one time known as Red Gravel Hills Road.

This is a substantial hike of over 12 miles round-trip.

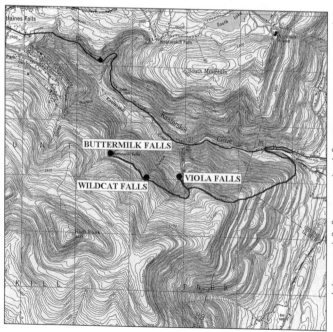

Maps created from TOPO!© National Geographic (www.nationalgeographic.com/topo)

Historic Waterfalls of
Upper Kaaterskill Clove

The upper section of Kaaterskill Clove beginning at the junction of Kaaterskill Creek and Lake Creek contains a number of large waterfalls culminating at the top of the clove with Haines Falls, the second largest cataract in the Catskills. Haines Falls, unfortunately, is located on private property owned by Twilight Park and is not open to the public.

The other falls are formed in dangerous, hard-to-reach recesses in the clove and have been inaccessible since the nineteenth-century heyday of the region's grand hotels. There is still much value in acknowledging the existence of these hidden waterfalls, however, since their stories are so much a part of the legends and lore of Kaaterskill Clove.

In his classic book, *The Catskill Mountain House*, Roland Van Zandt offers a brief description of what hiking through upper Kaaterskill Clove was like:

> [The gorge] becomes increasingly rough until washed out overhanging sides force the visitor to jump from rock to huge rock way in the middle of the creek, and an occasional gap must be crossed on a fallen, age-old tree. ... High overhead on the left hang the eyrie-like houses of Santa Cruz and Twilight Park perilously perched, or so it seems, directly above the void. Dripping Rock, constantly oozing water through its many crevices, towers high up on the right. At the foot of the old landslide, Triton Cave, Shelving Rock and finally Naiad's Bath become visible in their eerie beauty while the Five Cascades turn the scene into a fairyland with their constant rush of water in its ever changing sparkling beauty. But this is as far as the average visitor can go, since the old path on the left bank is completely washed away, and further penetration would require the use of ropes and possibly ladders.[1]

Naiad's Bath

Naiad's Bath is an attractive little falls and swimming hole.[1] The name, according to varied accounts, is derived from a poem written by a man named Armstrong, who proclaimed, "Come ye Naiads! to the fountains lead! Propitious maids! the task remains to sing."

The Five Cascades

Back in the 1800s, rustic ladders and walkways were mounted alongside the Five Cascades so that visitors could make their way cautiously up the ravine past obstacles. But none of these trappings remain, and the gorge is again as wild and dangerous as early explorers of the nineteenth century found it to be.[1-2]

A fascinating description of the Five Cascades can be found in Rev. Charles Rockwell's book, *The Catskill Mountains and the Region Around.* Rockwell begins his narration starting first with Haines Falls, and then proceeding downstream:

> The fall has two leaps, the first of one hundred and fifty feet, and the second of eighty, and the third one below of sixty feet, and others still, so that in less than one-fourth of a mile the stream falls four hundred and seventy-five feet. ... The falls are seven or eight in number; the third and fourth of them, from a narrow flood at their brink, spread in their descent over the sloping surfaces of the rocks, to a broad and minutely broken sheet at the base, like a web of pearl and silver gathered together at one end, in the hand, and suffered to flow over the surface of a terraced cone, in exquisite folds and fringes. At the foot of the fourth fall there is a covert of mossy and lichened coolness, all silver-starred with dew, roofed in by huge projecting tablets of rock, and at noon beautiful with an arched portal of rainbow. This is a place to stay and dream all day. The fifth fall is higher, and from it you can look backwards and see the whole succession of cataracts you have descended.[3]

The now-inaccessible Five Cascades, another favorite with 19th-century visitors.

Haines Falls

Haines Falls is an enormous cataract formed at the head of Kaaterskill Clove.[1] It was named after Charles W. Haines, who operated a mill on the stream above the fall. An old stone bridge leading to Twilight Park spans Kaaterskill Creek near the top of the fall, but Twilight Park, the bridge, and Haines Falls are all on private property and closed to the public.

In *Catskill Trails: A Ranger's Guide to the High Peaks,* Edward G. Henry puts the height of the falls at 180 feet.[2]

At the head of Kaaterskill Clove stands Haines Falls at 180 feet.

Around 1860, Charles W. Haines constructed a boardinghouse, which came to be known as the Haines Falls House, near the summit of the fall. Haines commercialized the falls, creating an elaborate network of ladders and wooden stairs leading down to the base of the waterfall. He also built a dam at the top, where controlled releases of water could be set into motion on cue in order to provide thrills to the paying tourists who stood eagerly watching from below. All of these embellishments are gone, returning the fall to its original state. For residents of Twilight Park and their guests, an observation deck along the south rim in the park provides a superb overlook of the waterfall.

A long-distance view of Haines Falls is possible by looking across Kaaterskill Clove from the escarpment trail southeast of Kaaterskill Falls.[3]

To access this view of Haines Falls, drive northwest on Rt. 23A to the village of Haines Falls. Turn right onto Rt. 18 (North Lake Road) and drive east for 2.2 miles. Turn right onto Schutt Road and drive south for about 200 feet. Pull into a parking area for hikers.

From the parking area follow the blue-blazed trail for 1.2 miles to Layman's Monument, crossing Lake Creek in the process. Between Layman's Monument and an overlook further southeast called Sunset Rock, you will have good views into the valley below and towards the head of Kaaterskill Clove where Haines Falls can be seen in the distance.

Lake Creek Area

Lake Creek is a medium-sized tributary that emanates from South Lake (a kettle lake that was formed during the last ice age) and flows into Kaaterskill Creek a short distance downstream from the famous horseshoe bend on Rt. 23A by Bastion Falls. Above Kaaterskill Falls, Lake Creek is joined by Spruce Creek, which contributes significantly to the flow of water going over the top of the falls.

There are two prominent falls on Lake Creek—Bastion Falls and the more renowned Kaaterskill Falls.

Bastion Falls

Accessibility: Roadside; 0.2-mile walk along the side of the road to the falls

Description: Bastion Falls is an absolutely marvelous roadside waterfall that brings traffic to a halt as drivers crane their necks to see the spectacle through their car windows as they pass by. The fall has also been called Rip Van Winkle Falls and was mistakenly identified in some turn-of-the-twentieth-century brochures as Sebastian Falls.

The huge, block shape cascade is roughly 50 feet high, with many drops and plunges.[1-2]

The ADK *Guide to Catskill Trails: Catskill Region* points out, emphatically, that "Bastion Falls is the cataract at the trailhead,"[3] and not Kaaterskill Falls. This point is well worth making, since several tour books (fortunately, not Catskill guidebooks) have mistakenly assumed that the fall at roadside was Kaaterskill Falls, or a lower section of it.[4]

Directions: Driving northwest through Kaaterskill Clove, you will eventually come to a dramatic horseshoe turn. The fall is located directly at the middle of this huge U-shaped turn, at roughly 3.4 miles from the intersection of Rtes. 23A & 32A in Palenville. Parking next to the fall is not permitted.

Continue around the bend and drive uphill for 0.2 mile. Just as the road curves to the right, you will see a large parking area on your left, which was once called Rip's Lookout. Pull in there and walk back down along the side of the road to the horseshoe turn, being very careful to keep to the side of the road. Cross over the bridge to where a path leads down to the base of the fall.

You can follow the yellow-blazed path up along the side of the cascade for views of the upper sections of the fall. The path is steep, however, and can be muddy and slippery.

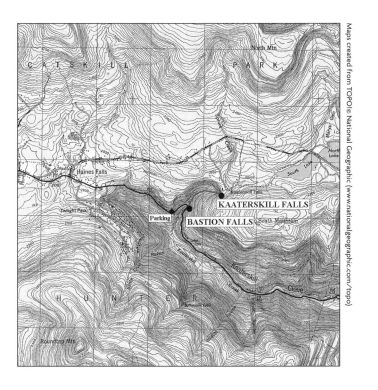

Maps created from TOPO!© National Geographic (www.nationalgeographic.com/topo)

Bastion Falls is guaranteed to bring cars to a crawl.

Kaaterskill Falls

Accessibility: 1.0-mile hike round-trip over uneven terrain, with steep ascent at the beginning of the trail **(See map on page 55.)**

Degree of Difficulty: Moderate

Description: Like Niagara Falls near Buffalo, and Taughannock Falls near Ithaca, Kaaterskill Falls is in a league all of its own. Once you see this waterfall, the image will remain with you forever.

Kaaterskill Falls consists of two large sections—an upper cataract 167 feet high, and a lower fall 64 feet in height. Altogether the falls stand 231 feet from top to bottom, making it one of the tallest waterfalls in New York State (some argue that it is the tallest).[1]

A little more than midway under the upper fall is an amphitheater that has formed because the sandstone and shale rock at the base of the falls wears away more quickly than the erosion-resistant Hamilton sandstone cap rock at the top of the falls. The immensity of this roofed cavity has to be seen to be appreciated![2-3]

In 1843, Thomas Cole, the first of the famous landscape artists from the Hudson River School, described the falls in an article that appeared in the *New York Evening Post:*

> There is a deep gorge in the midst of the loftiest Catskills, which, at its upper end, is terminated by a mighty wall of rock; as the spectator approaches from below, he sees its craggy and impending front rising to the height of three hundred feet. This huge rampart is semi-circular. From the center of the more distant or central part of the semi-circle, like a gush of living light from Heaven, the cataract leaps, and foaming into feathery spray, descends into a rocky basin one hundred and eighty feet below—thence the water flows over a platform forty or fifty feet, and precipitates itself over another rock eighty feet in height; then struggling and foaming through the shattered frag-

ments on the mountains, and shadowed by fantastic trees, it plunges into the gloomy depths of the valley below.[4]

A huge, inverted cone of ice slowly builds up under the upper falls in winter. According to Edward G. Henry in *Catskill Trails,* the column of ice can grow as high as 120 feet.[5]

The falls have been immortalized by the famous nineteenth-century poet, William Cullen Bryant, in a nineteen-stanza poem entitled Cauterskill Falls. The ninth stanza of the poem goes as follows:

'Tis only the torrent tumbling o'er,
In the midst of those glassy walls,
Gushing, and plunging, and beating the floor
Of the rocky basin in which it falls:
'Tis only the torrent—but why that start?
Why gazes the youth with a throbbing heart?[6]

History: There is a wealth of information about Kaaterskill Falls in numerous history and guidebooks. Not far from the top of the falls stood the Laurel House, a mountain hotel. It competed with the Catskill Mountain House and the Hotel Kaaterskill—two enormous, nearby mountain hotels—and managed to hold its own for over a century. The initial structure was built in 1852 by Peter Schutt. Sections were added on later until the Laurel House grew to over 100 rooms. The Laurel House dammed Lake Creek so a flow of water could be released over the falls (for payment) to please patrons if the season was dry. After many successful years followed by a slow decline, the hotel finally closed its doors in 1963, and in 1966 the property was purchased by the State of New York. The state deemed the building to be unsafe and not salvageable, and burned the structure to the ground in 1967. You can still see the ruins of old foundations if you search the area along the west bank, back from the top of the falls.

In the Laurel House's heyday, tourists could descend via catwalks and stairways from the top of the falls to the midsection. There, the upper, 167-foot-high plunge falls could be enjoyed, framed by its enormous amphitheater of rock that forms a semicircle behind the cataract.

Like any natural wonder that lures tourists like moths to a flame, the falls have seen their share of tragic accidents. Surprisingly, not all have been fatal. In 1850 a nineteen-year-old man from Utica fell off the top of the lower fall and tumbled into the basin, some 64 feet below. According to reports, a high freshet lessened the impact, and he survived with only a broken femur and fractured shoulder.

On another occasion a medium-sized dog belonging to the father of the owner of the Laurel House reportedly fell off the top of the upper falls. It tumbled 167 feet into the basin below, and yet was sufficiently unharmed that it was able to make its way up the steep slopes and back to the hotel. There have been no accounts, as far as we have been able to determine, of humans surviving a fall from the upper cataract at Kaaterskill Falls.

Directions: From the village of Palenville, follow Rt. 23A northwest up through Kaaterskill Clove towards the hamlet of Haines Falls. When you get to the horseshoe bend in Rt. 23A where Bastion Falls is visible at roadside, continue 0.2 mile until you reach a large parking area on the left. You will have driven approximately 3.6 miles from the junction of Rtes. 23A & 32A in Palenville.

From the parking area, walk back down to the horseshoe bend and Bastion Falls. Follow the yellow-blazed trail to Kaaterskill Falls, proceeding northeast. After an initial steep climb up the shoulder of Bastion Falls, the hike levels off substantially as it parallels the stream and gains elevation slowly. The trail is 0.5 mile long and ends at the base of the falls.

The pathway used to continue up the east slope next to the falls, leading to the huge amphitheater of the upper falls. This section of the path became heavily eroded, however; combined with the fact that there have been a number of lives lost at the upper fall's basin, it has been closed indefinitely.

You also may access the top of Kaaterskill Falls. Continue northwest along Rt. 23A from the parking area at Rip's Lookout to the hamlet of Haines Falls (a total of 4.9 miles from the intersection of Rtes. 23A & 32A). Turn right onto Rt. 18 (North Lake Road), which eventually leads to the campgrounds at North Lake. After you have gone

1.8 miles east along Rt. 18, turn right onto Laurel House Road and drive 0.4 mile south to its end. Park the car and follow a well-worn carriage road that leads to the top of the falls in just over 0.1 mile.

Don't venture out too close to the top of the falls. Several incautious hikers have fallen to their deaths from this spot.

The Laurel House once overlooked Kaaterskill Falls. Note the observation platform to the left at the top of the falls.

Ashley Falls

Location: Near Haines Falls (Greene County)

Accessibility: Less than 0.6-mile hike round-trip over uneven terrain; entrance fee required during camping season

Degree of Difficulty: Easy to Moderate

Description: Ashley Falls is formed on Ashley Creek, a small stream that rises on the southeastern shoulder of North Mountain and flows into North Lake roughly 0.5 mile below the falls.

The area containing the falls, Mary's Glen, has been well-known and frequently visited for the last two centuries because of the glen's close association with the Laurel House, Hotel Kaaterskill, and Catskill Mountain House. The three hotels provided lodging nearby to tourists by the thousands. All three are gone now, with only scant traces left behind.

Ashley Falls is roughly 40 feet high and consists of a 15-foot upper plunge fall and a lower cascade containing much talus, some of respectable size. At the upper, plunge fall, it is possible to walk out into the falling waters and cool off on a hot day.[1]

In *The Catskill Mountain House*, Roland Van Zandt states that "the falls are not large, but they are proportionate to the intimate seclusion of the surrounding dale and afford a delightful contrast to the more spectacular scenes of the upper trail."[2]

About 0.3 mile further up the red-blazed trail from Mary's Glen is a long escarpment ledge that produces a series of 6-foot-high waterfalls when sufficient water is flowing through the glen. Another 0.3 mile leads to a solitary cascade roughly 6 feet in height, this time formed as the stream rushes over a block of rock. Like the lower, ledge falls in the glen, it, too, is dependent on significant rainfall to produce an effect.

History: The falls are named after John Ashley who, in the 1790s, set up a number of log buildings near where Ashley Brook enters North Lake and began production of spruce beer (which was made from the "essence of spruce," water, sugar or molasses, and yeast, then allowed to ferment). As Ashley continued to harvest spruce trees for their tips, the forests around North Lake began to thin out. By 1809, Ashley's business had failed and the deforestation ended.[3]

Mary's Glen is named after Mary Scribner, wife of Ira Scribner who once operated a sawmill nearby. The glen is also referred to as Glen Mary. The site of the Scribner mill and house, called Glen Mary Cottage, may have been at the end of Schutt Road next to Lake Creek. The mill supplied lumber for the construction of the Catskill Mountain House, as well as other structures in the area.[4] Such illus-

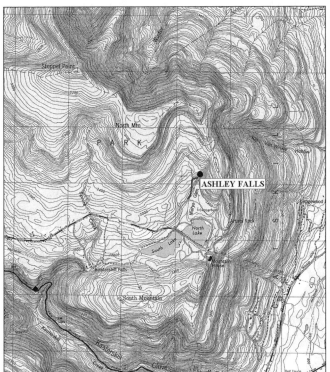

trious guests as Henry David Thoreau and William Ellery Channing reportedly stayed at the cottage. The Glen Mary Cottage failed to prosper after Peter Schutt commandeered the creek further downstream and diverted business to the Laurel House at the summit of Kaaterskill Falls.[5]

Directions: From Catskill take Rt. 23A southwest, wending your way through Palenville and up through Kaaterskill Clove. When you reach the hamlet of Haines Falls at 4.9 miles from the intersection of Rtes. 32A & 23A in Palenville, turn right onto Rt. 18 (North Lake Road), where signs direct you east towards the North-South Lake Campgrounds. After a drive of 2.3 miles, you will reach the entrance gate at the North-South Lake Campgrounds. Be prepared to pay an entrance fee during the summer season. Continue straight along the main road, going east for roughly 0.2 mile. When you reach the point where the road divides and one section goes to the right down a steep hill, continue straight ahead, following a sign indicating the way to the Picnic Area. You will soon come to a trail marker on your left for Mary's Glen, just before you cross over a tiny bridge that spans Ashley Creek. You will have traveled about 0.9 mile from the tollgate.

The trail to Mary's Glen involves a hike of under 0.3 mile along a fairly level, but rock-strewn pathway. The best views of Ashley Falls are from the bottom and midway up.

If you continue along the red-blazed trail proceeding uphill from the top of Ashley Falls another 0.4 mile, you will come to a series of smaller falls along an escarpment ridge. The falls are located where the yellow-blazed trail, connecting the North Lake Gatehouse to Badman's Cave, crosses the red-blazed trail. Take note that if you are hiking this trail during the dry season, you are likely to see little of the falls, if anything at all.

If you continue hiking uphill on the red-blazed trail for another 0.2-0.3 miles, you will come to a small, block-shaped cascade to your right. This fall also tends to be lackluster unless you are visiting during the rainy season.

Platte Clove

Platte Clove is a wild, untamed, stupendous mountain pass that is breathtaking to behold from roadside and from the trails along its rim, but dangerous if you attempt to descend into its depths. In *Hiking the Catskills,* Lee McAllister describes the clove as one of the most rugged areas in the eastern United States. I would have to agree.

An article written in *Harper's New Monthly Magazine* in 1883, entitled "The Catskills," states: "the cloves are many, and I think that known as the Platterkill is the wildest and most picturesque, but only hardy walkers should attempt its ascent. Eighteen waterfalls may be counted in a walk up this clove, and the wild grandeur of the scene has defied almost every pen and pencil."[1] The reason why such caution is recommended is that within the span of less than two miles, the clove rises from an elevation of 700 feet to 2,200 feet, boxed in by enormous walls descending from Kaaterskill High Peak to the north and Plattekill and Overlook Mountains to the south. There are many high precipices and vertical heights where incautious bushwhackers could topple off into the void.

The number of waterfalls contained in the gorge is subject to some interpretation, depending upon one's particular system for determining exactly what constitutes a waterfall, and also depending upon whether waterfalls on tributaries are counted. In *Guide to the Catskills,* 10 major waterfalls are listed: Black Chasm Falls, Plaatkill Falls, Old Mill Falls, Pomeroy Falls, Rainbow Falls, Lower Rainbow Falls, Green Falls (also known as The Ghost), Evergreen Falls, Rocky Rapids, and Gray Rock Falls.[2] In *Catskill Trails,* Edward G. Henry writes that "within its reaches are 14 waterfalls higher than 20 feet."[3]

Most of the main waterfalls are formed on the Plattekill, a medium-sized stream that rises on the southern shoulder of Kaaterskill High Peak and flows into the Esopus Creek near Glenerie Falls at Glenerie. Geologically the Plattekill is a fairly youthful stream. Several waterfalls are also formed on tributaries, including those on Hell's Hole Creek.

According to Edward Henry, Platte Clove is divided into two

distinct sections: the upper and lower. In the upper section, waterfalls are tall and terrifying, the terrain is more chiseled, and the side
walls are nearly vertical. It is a segment whose V-shaped walls are
suggestive of the aftermath of a high-impacting stream, rather than
the residual effects of glaciers. In the clove's lower, or bottom section, the stream has become more placid and the terrain less formidable, with a number of waterfalls, but none greater than 25 feet in
height. This is a segment whose contoured, U-shaped walls are characterized more by the effects of the last glacier than the stream currently cutting through it.[4]

One of the first Europeans to hike through Platte Clove was
Peter de Labigarre who, in 1793, after hiking up to Overlook
Mountain, figured that the pass would provide a quick and easy
route back down into the valley. The hike proved to be not so easy.
Labigarre later described the head of the clove as a place where the
mountain was split asunder, and the gorge itself was a "horrid
place." He was by no means the first European to travel through the
clove, however. In 1776, during the Revolutionary War, Captain
Jeremiah Snyder and his 18-year-old son, Elias, were captured by
Indians and Tories and taken through Platte Clove on their way to
Fort Niagara. It must have been quite a trip![5]

R. Lionel De Lisser, in *Picturesque Catskills: Greene County,*
describes a hike down through Platte Clove:

> After a visit to Black Chasm and Plaaterskill Falls, the
> next point of interest is the Old Mill Falls, just below the
> bridge that crosses the stream on the Overlook Mountain
> Road.
>
> Then comes Pomeroy Falls. ... The next fall below
> Pomeroy is the Rainbow, the one below that is the Lower
> Rainbow, or Hell Hole Falls. The stream that enters the
> creek at this point comes from High Peak, passes under
> Hells Hole bridge, on the clove wagon road, and falls
> almost perpendicularly hundreds of feet, over huge rocks
> and high cliffs, into the wild stream below.
>
> Green Falls come next. A second view of this falls I
> have called "The Ghost."... Evergreen Falls is named from

the quantities of green moss that covers its rocks, and comes next in order. Then comes Rocky Rapids, which is a wild and rather a dangerous spot, quite narrow and in which one is in much danger from the rocks hanging above as from the big boulders in the path. Gray Rock is a beautiful falls. ... the stream from Black Chasm enters the creek just below these falls.

The last falls in Greene County is the Upper Red Falls, so called to distinguish it from the Lower Red Falls, which is in Ulster County."[6]

Here, De Lisser is making the point that lower Platte Clove is bisected by the line that separates Greene County from Ulster County.

There are excellent views into Platte Clove from Huckleberry Point (a hike that can be found in any number of guidebooks dealing with the Catskills), but none that reveals the awesome depths of the gorge and its waterfalls.

Platte Clove was well known to artists of the Hudson River School, although the clove was never captured on canvas with the same frequency and degree of intimacy as was Kaaterskill Clove. Charles Lanman was one of the first artists to venture into Platte Clove (which he referred to as Plauterkill Clove) for subject matter, but he was hardly the last. Lanman made his headquarters near the foot of Platte Clove at the Dutch farmhouse of Levi Myer. This gave him a decided advantage over other artists, whose base of operations was generally north of Kaaterskill Clove at one of the three mountain hotels. According to Lanman, the clove abounded "in waterfalls of surpassing beauty, varying ten to a hundred and fifty feet in height, whose rocks are green with the moss of centuries."

At one time, some consideration was given to opening up Platte Clove and its mighty waterfalls by using the Overlook Mountain House on Overlook Mountain as a point of entry, in much the same way that Kaaterskill Clove was made accessible by its three mountain houses, but this never came to pass.[7-9]

Directions: From I-87 (the NYS Thruway) get off at Exit 20 for Saugerties, and go west on Rt. 212 for 2.4 miles. At Centerville turn right onto Rt. 35 (Blue Mountain Road) and drive north for 1.4 miles. You will come to a fork in the road. Veer to the left, taking Rt. 33,

Platte Clove remains wild and difficult to access today.
The narrow, winding road through the clove is not maintained
in the winter months.

and proceed due west until you reach the village of West Saugerties. Continue through the village and cross over a stone bridge that spans Plattekill Creek (Note: Schalk's Falls can be seen upstream from the bridge). Within 0.4 mile you will come to the beginning of a paved, seasonal road (not maintained from November 15–April 15) called Platte Clove Road, which leads up into Platte Clove. Do not try to access this road during the winter. Platte Clove Road has no guardrails. Vertical drop-offs to the south have only a smattering of loosely held trees to stop your car from tumbling hundreds of feet to the bottom of the gorge!

Drive uphill on Platte Clove Road, which will take you high above the Plattekill and the huge gorge that looms on the south side of your vehicle. This is not a trip for the faint of heart. The drive has a perilous feel to it. There are many places, as you twist and turn, where little separates you and the road from a drop-off of many hundreds of feet into the gorge below. The road has been in service since its construction in the 1880s, however, and many thousands of people have traveled on it. Drive prudently and do not attempt to take the road in bad weather, and you will be as safe as on almost any other highway.

Start clocking the mileage from the bridge spanning the Plattekill at Schalk's Falls, 0.4 mile before you come to where the road is seasonal. At 1.7 miles you will negotiate a wide horseshoe turn where the views are incredible. At 2.3 miles, near the top of the clove, you will come to a parking area on your left just before you cross an old stone bridge. You have now reached the area known as Hell's Hole and the Devil's Kitchen.

If you prefer not to drive up through Platte Clove, bear in mind that it is also possible to reach the top of the clove by taking Rt. 23A west from Catskill through Kaaterskill Clove. Drive through Haines Falls and Tannersville. About a mile before you get to Rt. 214 and Hunter Mountain, turn left onto Bloomer Road and continue southeast on Rt. 16 until you reach the top of Platte Clove, where a sign ahead warns of proceeding further during the "off season." Park in the area to your right, just past the stone bridge.

Assuming that you are driving up from the bottom of Platte Clove, we'll begin our tour with Schalk's Falls.

Schalk's Falls

Accessibility: Roadside

Description: This 8-foot-high waterfall is formed on Plattekill Creek just down from the base of Platte Clove. Here the Plattekill arrives from the west, falls into an obliquely oriented ravine, and veers off momentarily to the north before resuming its eastward course of direction.

Directions: From West Saugerties head west towards the entrance to Platte Clove. At 0.4 mile before the beginning of the clove, where a sign points out that this is a seasonal road and warns of proceeding any further off-season, stop at an old stone bridge spanning the Plattekill. The falls are just upstream, quite visible from the top of the bridge.

If you look down from the north side the bridge, you will notice that the narrow chasm continues downstream from the falls, forming several tiny cascades before it rounds the bend and begins heading east again.

Shalk's Falls at the bottom of Platte Clove.

Hell's Hole

Accessibility: Roadside

Description: Hell's Hole is an awesome gulf with precipitous walls and boulders of monstrous size that delves into Platte Clove beginning at the point where Platte Clove Mountain Road crosses over Hell's Hole Creek.

There are three small waterfalls formed in the nearby section of Hell's Hole. All are formed on Hell's Hole Creek, a small stream that rises on the southern shoulder of Kaaterskill High Peak (elevation 3655') and enters the Plattekill at the bottom of the gulf. The tiny stream that you see today gives little evidence of the mighty fury that once flowed down this ravine helping to carve out in ancient times what has become the Hell's Hole of today.

From the top of the stone bridge, you can view two small falls upstream and one small waterfall downstream. Looking upstream, the first waterfall is located close to the foot of the bridge. It is fissure-created—the water has sliced through the streambed, forming a 4-foot drop. The second waterfall, further upstream, is broader and also 4 feet in height. A huge, table-like rock rests on its eastern flank, forming a shelter cave at the base of the cascade.

Directly south of the bridge, looking almost straight down you will be able to see a narrow channel where the water is squeezed and shoots out, creating a cascade four to five feet in height.[1-2]

History: The falls are located at the top of Hell's Hole, next to an area called the Devil's Kitchen. The Devil's Kitchen consists of a conglomeration of huge boulders strewn about on top of an enormous platform of rock. They are the aftermath of the last glacier. In *The Catskills: From Wilderness to Woodstock*, Alf Evers writes: "These boulders were the Devil's saucepans, his tea kettle, and other pieces of kitchenware. Ladders and stairways would lead from one level to another. The guide would give details of the Devil's

Devil's Kitchen, Platte Clove,
Catskill Mts., N. Y.

75-64

Falls at Hell's Hole.

methods of cooking and point out his many ingenious household gadgets. ... Vacationers were happy to pay their dimes to spend a half hour of mock horror among the Devil's pots and pans and to feel superior to the old-timers who had taken such things seriously."[3] None of the rustic ladders or walkways, or the gazebo survives today.

A summer hotel, called the Plattekill Falls Mountain House, once stood at the head of the clove and provided lodging to those wishing to linger and explore the clove more fully. In the late 1800s it was owned and operated by H. V. Leaycraft. Buildings at the rear of the hotel featured caged animals such as black bears, raccoons, and foxes.

A terrifyingly steep slope descends into the maw of the gulf. Truly there is no other place in the region quite like this, where nature seems both terrifying and sublime in its awesome majesty.

Directions: Hell's Hole is located at the top of the clove where Rt. 16 crosses over an old, picturesque stone bridge. Driving up from West Saugerties through Platte Clove, turn into a small parking area on your left just as you seemingly crest the top of the clove. If you reach the stone bridge, then you have gone too far. Take note of the posted signs next to the parking area, which prohibit entry to a massive, high overlook where Hell's Hole Creek and the Plattekill join.

Old Mill Falls

Accessibility: Short hike over uneven terrain

Degree of Difficulty: Easy

Description: Old Mill Falls is formed on the Plattekill just below where a historic bridge once crossed the creek. A new bridge, built in 2001, now spans the stream at the same spot.

The falls consist of two ledges with a total drop of over 10 feet.[1]

History: In the late 1880s a well-constructed king post bridge, which came to be known as the Overlook Bridge, was built just above the falls. That bridge survived until approximately 1920. The new bridge, striving for historical accuracy, was modeled after the original bridge and even uses the surviving stone abutments that supported its predecessor. The original Overlook Bridge, however, was significantly wider than the current footbridge. It had to accommodate the weight of stagecoaches transporting passengers up to the Plattekill Falls House or Overlook Mountain House, as well as wagons carrying bluestone from rock quarries on the mountain slopes to the south.

Because of its ready accessibility, the falls were frequently visited by guests at the Overlook Mountain House, and by travelers making their way from one mountain house to the other or from the valley below.

Old Mill Falls is now part of the Platte Clove Preserve, and the section of the trail containing it is part of the turquoise-blazed Long Path.

Directions: From the stone bridge overlooking the Devil's Kitchen near the top of the clove, drive west on Platte Clove Road for 0.2 mile. Look for a sign on your left indicating the Platte Clove Preserve, where green markers are evident. You will see a small pull-off to your left at this point. This is the trailhead to the preserve.

Follow the trail down to the stream and cross over the Plattekill. The falls are directly downstream, easily within view.

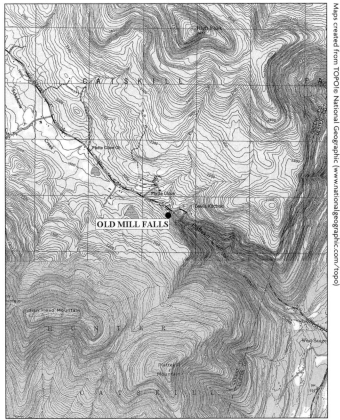

Plattekill Falls near the head of Platte Clove.

Plattekill Falls

Accessibility: 0.4-mile hike round-trip

Degree of Difficulty: Easy to Moderate

Description: Plattekill Falls is a large, plunging waterfall exceeding 70 feet in height, formed near the top of the clove. It is contained in a section of the ravine where steep walls loom to the south and sloping walls extend to the north. Just above the top of the waterfall are several small cascades that are not visible from below.

In *Catskill Rambles*, Kenneth Wapner writes, "I'd been contemplating the waterfall at the head of Platteclove—falling without

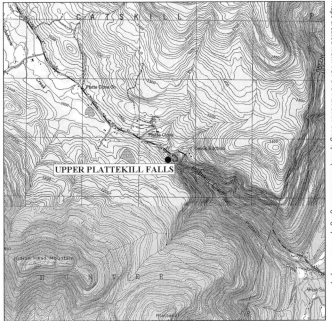

UPPER PLATTEKILL FALLS

pause, ceaselessly dropping, but to my eye oddly static. I thought of the Taoist precept: The waterfall fills the pool above as well as below."[1] This is a great spot for meditation. There is even a large, flat rock in the middle of the stream near the base of the falls where you can perch and gaze close-up upon this marvelous construct of nature.

Directions: From the parking area in front of the trailhead for the Platte Clove Preserve, walk back east along the road for less than 50 feet and follow a driveway that leads off to the right, going past a red-colored cabin maintained by the Platte Clove Preserve. Stay on this dirt road, which quickly turns into a path, and follow it downhill, making a large U-turn at one point that will bring you down to the base of Plattekill Falls, several hundred feet lower in elevation than the cabin.

This beautiful hike is no more than 0.2 mile in length and leads you to one of the Catskills' most spectacular waterfalls.

Stony Clove

Stony Clove is a fascinating mountain pass that has cut a notch over 1,400 feet deep into one of the highest regions of the central escarpment. In the clove's most constricted section, the west wall rises up over 1,000 feet and then continues on an upwards slope towards Hunter Mountain for over another 1,000 feet of elevation; to the east, the walls rise up to over 1,200 feet.[1]

The pass drains the southwestern slopes of three, very high mountain peaks: Hunter Mountain, second highest in the Catskills at 4,040 feet; West Kill Mountain at 3,880 feet; and Plateau Mountain at 3,840 feet.

When you park at the Devil's Tombstone Campsite at Stony Clove, be sure to visit the Devil's Tombstone, a sandstone monolith measuring 5 x 7 feet that has been a favorite photo subject since the mid-1800s and an ongoing item of curiosity.

The Devil's Tombstone is near the trailhead.

Fall in Becker Hollow

Location: Hunter Mountain (Greene County)

Accessibility: 0.8-mile hike round-trip, fairly level

Degree of Difficulty: Easy

Description: This unnamed waterfall, consisting of two ledge falls dropping a total of 8 feet, is formed on a tiny creek that passes through Becker Hollow. The stream rises on the east slope of Hunter Mountain and flows into Schoharie Creek.

At the top of the fall, a long, breached cement dam can be observed. Aluminum water pipes lie scattered about, revealing a past much different from today's rustic setting.

History: According to Edward G. Henry, in *Catskill Trails,* the old road passing by the fall leads to a long-deserted farmstead.[1] This property was owned by a man named Becker whose family lived in the area for many years, according to Peter Kick in *Catskill Mountain Guide.*[2] Becker's oldest son became a forest fire observer and was stationed along with his family at the fire tower on top of Hunter Mountain during the 1920s. Becker, like so many other farmers in the Catskills, tirelessly worked the rocky land to grow crops for family sustenance, and to feed the townsfolk who worked the mills and their horses. But the soil was too infertile to sustain crops for any length of time, and gradually most of the farms in the Catskills, including Becker's, were abandoned. Today all that remain are rock walls and collapsing stone foundations.

Hunter Mountain was named after John Hunter, a landowner who lived in the mid-1880s.

Directions: Driving west past Tannersville on Rt. 23A, turn left onto Rt. 214. Drive south for 1.2 miles and pull in at the trailhead parking for Hunter Mountain.

Follow the blue-blazed trail through a huge stone arch, and begin walking west. In 0.3 mile you will cross over a footbridge. Within another 0.1 mile you will come to the fall, which will be on your left. There are several paths leading from the trail to the fall. One takes you to the base; another takes you right across the top of the dam.

If you were to continue on the blue-blazed trail for another 2 miles, climbing steadily uphill, you would reach the summit of Hunter Mountain, which at 4,040 feet is the second highest peak in the Catskill Mountains.

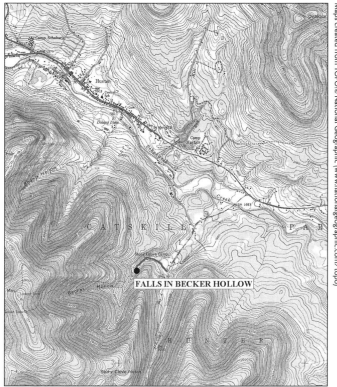

Falls in Stony Notch

Location: Near Hunter (Greene County)

Accessibility: 0.6-mile hike round-trip

Degree of Difficulty: Moderate; slight 0.2-mile bushwhack following a stream uphill

Description: This series of cascading falls is formed in a small notch on the southwest slope of Plateau Mountain. The stream containing the cascades quickly flows into Stony Creek not far from Notch Lake. The falls are narrow, dropping for about 15 feet as they flow over green moss.

The falls are on a small creek, so be sure to visit when plenty of water is flowing, such as in early spring.

Directions: From Tannersville, turn left onto Rt. 214 and drive south for roughly 3 miles. Park at the south end of Notch Lake at the Devil's Tombstone Campsite after paying for a day-use ticket. (Note: This fee is required only if you are visiting during the camping season.)

Cross the road, walk up a small flight of stairs formed out of logs, and begin hiking up the red-blazed Devil's Tombstone Trail towards Plateau Mountain, some 3.2 miles distant. After 0.1 mile, veer off to the right on a faint, side trail that quickly leads to a small stream. Follow the stream uphill for no more than 0.2 mile and you will be at the cascades.

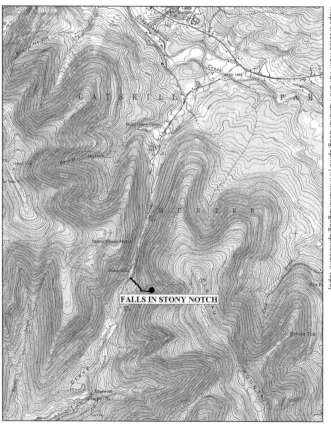

FALLS IN STONY NOTCH

Maps created from TOPO!® National Geographic (www.nationalgeographic.com/topo)

Diamond Notch Falls

Location: Near Hunter (Greene County)

Accessibility: 4.6-mile hike round-trip over uneven terrain

Difficulty: Moderate to Difficult

Description: Diamond Notch Falls is formed on the Westkill, a medium-sized stream that rises on the south slopes of Hunter Mountain and flows into Schoharie Creek at Lexington. The waterfall is roughly 10 feet high and is well worth seeing regardless of whether there is a high stream flow or the creek is just a trickle. A footbridge spans the creek just upstream from the falls.

The falls also have been known as Westkill Falls and Buttermilk Falls. Several hundred feet downstream from the main falls is a second waterfall approximately 4 feet in height.[1-4]

Directions: Take Rt. 23A west out of Catskill, drive through Palenville, and continue west on Rt. 23A past Tannersville. Turn left onto Rt. 214 (a major route heading south towards Phoenicia) and drive south for 7.2 miles to Lanesville, along the way passing by the Devil's Tombstone at 3.2 miles. Turn right onto Diamond Notch Road and drive north for 1.1 miles. At this point the road becomes rough and bumpy. Continue on, if you can, for another 0.4 mile to where limited trailhead parking is available.

Proceed straight ahead on foot through Diamond Notch Hollow following a trail that parallels Hollow Tree Brook. The trail was developed in 1937 to be used as a backcountry ski trail between Lanesville (in Stony Clove) and Spruceton (west of Hunter Mountain). At 1.5 miles into the hike, you will see a tiny waterfall off to your right. At 2.3 miles you will reach the junction with the red-blazed Devil's Path. When you come to the bridge, you will be directly above the fall. Just before the footbridge is a tiny path that veers off to the left, which you can follow down to the base of the fall.

There is an alternate approach that requires a longer drive, but a shorter hike. From Tannersville continue west on Rt. 23A for over 12 miles. When you come to Lexington (junction of Rtes. 23A & 42), turn left onto Rt. 42 and drive south for 4.1 miles. Turn left onto Spruceton Road (Rt. 6) and drive east for 7 miles, paralleling the south bank of the West Kill. Pass by the first parking area (on your left). When you reach the cable barrier, park in the area provided at the end of the road.

Follow the blue-blazed Spruceton Trail southeast for 0.7 mile to the fall.

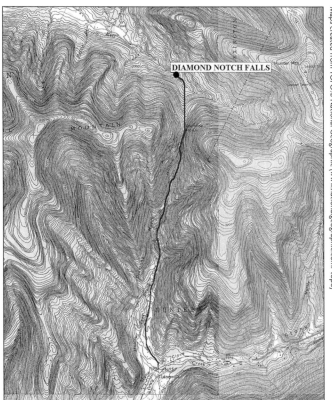

Falls on the Roaring Kill

Location: Near Tannersville (Greene County)

Accessibility: 0.1-mile hike round-trip along faint path following bank of the Roaring Kill

Degree of Difficulty: Easy

Description: There are several small but pretty cascades formed on the Roaring Kill, a medium-sized stream that rises between Sugarloaf Mountain and Spruce Top, and flows into nearby Schoharie Creek. In descending order, going downstream, you will encounter two, 3-foot cascades followed by a lovely 4-foot cascade that is bearded with green moss.

The stream is replete with huge boulders, making it a very scenic place to stop and linger, or to cool off if you have just finished a hike up Twin or Sugarloaf mountains.

Directions: The turnoff for Twin Mountain can be approached from two directions. Coming from the east on Rt. 16 through Platte Clove, continue west past the Platte Clove Preserve for 1.7 miles, then turn left onto Dale Road. From Tannersville, continue west on Rt. 23A for over 1.5 miles, and then turn left onto Bloomer Road (which turns into Platte Clove Mountain Road—Rt. 16). Drive southeast for 4.5 miles, then turn right onto Dale Road.

From either direction, drive south on Dale Road for 0.6 mile and then turn right onto Roaringkill Road. Follow Roaringkill southwest for 0.6 mile until you reach the trailhead parking for Twin Mountain.

From the parking area walk down the dirt road for 0.05 mile to a newly constructed bridge that spans the Roaring Kill. From the bridge you can look downstream and see several small cascades. By following a faint path paralleling the stream downstream from the north end of the bridge, you can visit the cascades close up.

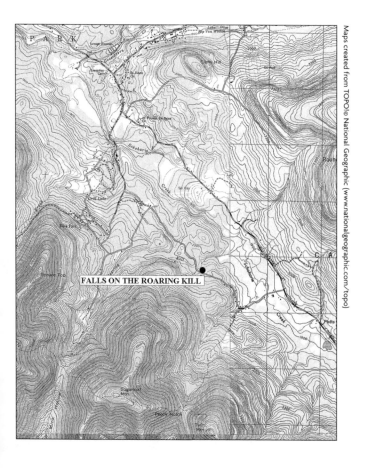

FALLS ON THE ROARING KILL

Fall on the Eastkill

Location: Near Tannersville (Greene County)

Accessibility: 6.0-mile hike round-trip

Degree of Difficulty: Moderate to Difficult

Description: This enchanting, 8-foot-high waterfall is formed on the Eastkill, a small tributary that rises in the hills north of Stoppel Point and flows into the Schoharie Creek at Jewett Center.[1] Along the way the Eastkill is impounded at Lake Capra and Colgate Lake.[2]

There are excellent views to the north of the Thomas Cole, Black Dome, and Black Head mountains. When you reach the open spaces of Spruce Woods, where a settlement once existed, you will find (as Doris West Brooks observed years ago) that "the sheer size of the field is startling."[3]

History: The waterfall is located in Spruce Woods, an area of historic significance where a community of sawyers and woodcutters grew up around a common mill. The hamlet has been gone for many years, and there is little to show that civilization ever domesticated this area, save for the outline of the old road, a few crumbling foundations, and traces of relics from the past.[4]

The trail leading to Spruce Woods was once part of the East Jewett-Catskill Turnpike, which led from East Jewett through Dutchers Pass and down to Round Top. In the nineteenth century this proved to be the shortest route for Jewett Valley farmers to get their produce to the village of Catskill, where it then could be shipped to other ports along the Hudson River.

Colgate Lake, near where you will park, is named after the Colgate Palmolive-Peet Company magnate, Robert Colgate, who once owned much of the land in the area.

Directions: From the junction of Rtes. 23A & 32A in Palenville, proceed west on Rt. 23A for 7.0 miles into Tannersville. Turn right onto Rt. 23C and drive north for 3.1 miles, passing by Onteora Park in the process. You also will pass by an impressive old stone church (the Onteora Chapel) to your right where Rt. 25 comes in. When you get to Colgate Road (Rt. 78) in East Jewett, turn right and proceed east. At 1.4 miles from the intersection of Rtes. 23C & 78, you will pass by the outlet dam at Colgate Lake. At 1.7 miles you will reach the parking area for Dutchers Notch, which will be on your left.

Hike the trail north from the parking lot for 0.2 mile to the edge of the woods. From here stay on the yellow-blazed footpath as it continues north and then turns west. Note that the trail will abruptly change direction a number of times. Stay alert, however, and you will do fine, for this is a very well-marked, well-maintained

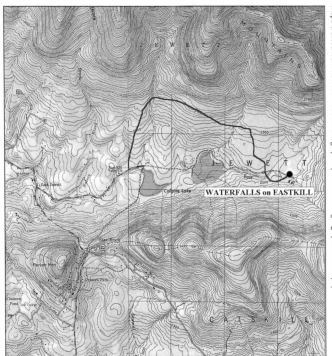

WATERFALLS on EASTKILL

footpath. At 1.2 miles you will cross over a wide footbridge that spans a small tributary to Lake Capra. From here the hike generally proceeds in a southeast direction. After 1.8 miles you will cross over a footbridge spanning a tributary of the Eastkill.

Eventually you will come to a large, open expanse of land that is part swamp and part lake. The trail veers around this area. Soon you will cross over a third footbridge, at the Eastkill outlet to the swampy lake. Look closely and you will notice that the footbridge was constructed on top of the stone abutments of an earlier bridge. This earlier bridge, along with the stone arch bridge that you will see on your left just further up the trail, hearken back to an earlier time when the area supported a thriving community and was well traveled by horse teams pulling wagon loads of goods.

When you come to the fourth footbridge, at a distance of 2.9 miles, you will cross over the Eastkill again and walk into an enormous open field where the settlement of Spruce Woods once stood. Follow the yellow-blazed trail, now paralleling the north bank of the Eastkill, west for 0.1 mile and you will see the fall, off to your right in the woods.

If you enjoy winter outings, take note that the trail also is suitable for snowshoeing and cross-country skiing.

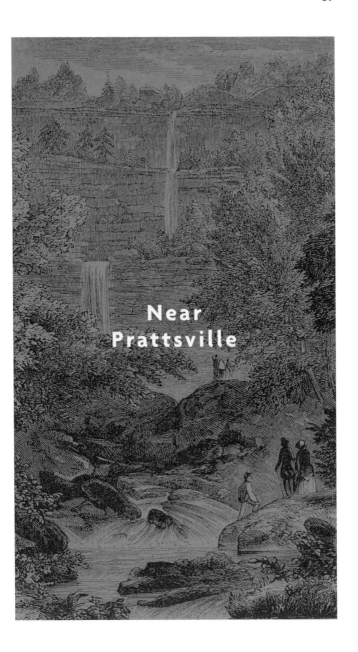

Near
Prattsville

Red Falls

Location: Near Prattsville (Greene County)

Accessibility: Roadside

Description: Red Falls consists of a series of ledges and cascades formed on the Bataviakill, a medium-sized stream that rises near Blackhead Mountain and flows into Schoharie Creek several miles west of the falls. The falls are fairly broad, stair-like, and roughly 30 feet in height.[1-2]

According to J. Van Vechten Vedder, in *History of Greene County, New York, 1651-1800*, the town and waterfall received its name "from the falls and the peculiar color of its waters which flow over red sandstone."[3]

History: By the year 1829, Foster Morss had purchased a gristmill, sawmill, and a shingle factory near the waterfall. Soon after, a tannery was added, which quickly became the dominant industry. The tanning industry spread rapidly from the villages of Red Falls and adjacent Prattsville to Tannersville and a number of other nearby mountain towns. For half a century the Catskills were a prominent, world-renowned tannery region, until deforestation finally brought the industry to a grinding halt.[4]

Foster Morss apparently also owned a cotton mill, which survived until 1881,[5] and according to Francis P. Kimball, in *The Capital Region of New York State*, "Jay Gould made his first money in cotton at Red Falls."[6]

The village of Red Falls was once known as Federal City.

Directions: From I-87 (the NYS Thruway) get off at Exit 21 for Catskill, and proceed west on Rt. 23 for around 30 miles. If you pass by Red Falls without realizing it (since it faces in the opposite direction), you soon will come to the junction of Rtes. 23 & 23A. Simply turn around and backtrack for 1.5 miles to the falls.

There is a roadside pull-off near the top of the fall. From here, walk west on Rt. 23 for a short distance to view the fall from roadside.

Additional Points of Interest: Red Falls is very close to the famous Pratt Rock Park in Prattsville. Pratt Rock was built by Zadock Pratt, the founder of Prattsville, who was a wealthy, although somewhat eccentric, businessman. Pratt Rock is a collection of stone carvings etched in the mid-1850s into the rock face of a towering escarpment some 500 feet above the road. *Ripley's Believe It or Not* once referred to Pratt Rock as "New York's Mt. Rushmore."

The park is located along Rt. 23, about 0.5 miles northwest of the junction of Rtes. 23 & 23A.

Red Falls, named for the color of its rocks.

Hardenbergh Falls

Location: Near Prattsville (Greene County)

Accessibility: Roadside

Description: Hardenbergh Falls is formed on the Bear Kill, a small stream issuing from Mayham Pond near South Gilboa and flowing directly into the Schoharie Reservoir near the base of the falls.

The waterfall is roughly 20 feet high and drops into a fairly spacious, wide open area at the edge of the Schoharie Reservoir. Hardenbergh also has been spelled Hardenburg and Hardenburgh in the past.[1-2]

History: Hardenbergh Falls presumably was named after Major Johannis Hardenbergh, who received a two million-acre tract of land in 1708 called the Hardenbergh Patent. One of his descendants, a Miss Hardenbergh, owned a colonial homestead near the falls.

Directions: From Prattsville, set the odometer to zero as you cross the northwest end of the bridge leaving town, proceed west for 1.5 miles along Rt. 23, then turn right (northeast) onto an unmarked, but well-maintained dirt road (which is listed on the *NYS Gazetteer* as Intake Road) and drive north for 0.2 mile. You will go down a steep hill and cross over a small bridge.

Park immediately to the side after crossing over the Bear Kill. The fall is below, down from the east side of the bridge, and should be viewed from roadside unless you have an access permit.

Hardenbergh Falls now drops into the Schoharie Reservoir.

Near
Margaretville

Margaretville is near the eastern end of the Pepacton
Reservoir and is located at the western boundary
of the Catskill Park between towering 2,600-foot-high
Pakatakan Mountain to the south and
2,211-foot-high Kettle Hill to the north.
Margaretville is named after Margaret Lewis—
the daughter of Governor Morgan Lewis and the great-
granddaughter of Johannes Hardenbergh, for whom
Hardenbergh Falls at Grand Gorge was named.[1]

Bushnellville Creek Falls

Location: Near Bushnellville (Greene County)

Accessibility: Roadside

Description: This beautiful cascade is formed on a tiny tributary to Bushnellville Creek, a small stream that rises from Halcott Mountain and flows into the Esopus Creek at Shandaken.

The waterfall is over 40 feet high and located near the end of Deep Notch, one of three mountain passes that was cut through the central escarpment. Deep Notch has been a main passageway for glaciers and streams. At the end of the notch, at Shandaken, can be found signs of a large, ancient delta, visible to the discerning eyes of geologists.

The parking area next to the fall is used frequently by hikers setting out on a bushwhack to the top of Halcott Mountain (elevation 3,537 feet) in a quest to become a "35er" and to join the rapidly expanding population of hikers who have climbed every mountain in the Catskills 3,500 feet or more in height.

Bear in mind that this waterfall often runs dry, so visit during the rainy season.

History: Bushnellville was named after Captain Aaron Bushnell, an early settler and gristmill owner.

The notch has been known as Westkill Notch and Shandaken Notch, as well as Deep Notch, and is formed between Halcott Mountain to the west and Balsam Mountain to the east.

Directions: Take Exit 19 for Kingston off the NYS Thruway and drive west on Rt. 28 for roughly 27 miles. When you come to Shandaken (junction of Rtes. 28 & 42), turn right onto Rt. 42 and drive north for 5.0 miles. You will see the fall to your left. Immediately after the fall, pull into a large parking area on the left side of the road.

If approaching from the north (junction of Rtes. 23A and 42 near Lexington), drive south on Rt. 42 for around 6.5 miles. The fall will be directly to your right, following a large pull-off on the right-hand side of the road.

Dry Brook Falls

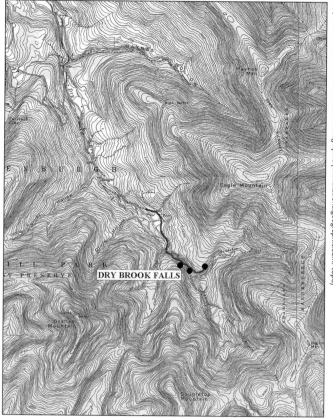

Dry Brook Falls

Location: Near Arkville (Ulster County)

Accessibility: 2.6-mile hike round-trip along a well-maintained trail
(See map on facing page.)

Degree of Difficulty: Moderate

Description: There are three small falls to be enjoyed along this hike: two are formed on Dry Brook, a small stream that rises west of Big Indian Mountain and flows into the East Branch of the Delaware River at Arkville; the third is a set of falls formed on Shandaken Brook, a small stream that rises north of Big Indian Mountain and flows into Dry Brook.[1]

The first waterfall encountered is on Dry Brook. The fall is a 6-foot-high, gently inclined cascade. At its bottom a pool has formed near Dry Brook's confluence with Flatiron Creek.[2]

The second waterfall is also on Dry Brook, and consists of an 8-foot-high fall formed in a tiny chasm and spanned by a bridge crossing its top. A large buttress of rock stands to the side of the waterfall, showing signs of continuous erosion on all sides when the stream swells and flows around the massive obstruction.[3]

The third waterfall is formed on Shandaken Brook and is contained in a fairly rugged, deeply cut chasm. The chasm, which extends for well over several hundred feet, contains a 10-foot cascade near the downstream end and a 6-foot cascade at the very bottom where the chasm abruptly turns into an undistinguished ravine.

History: Dry Brook is a corruption of the German words *drei brucke,* which translates to "three bridges." One of the bridges, called the Forge Bridge, was built in 1906.[4]

Hiram Seager built the first mill on the upper section of the stream. Seager Trail is named for this early settler. In the 1860s,

Hiram D. Cook built a sawmill at a point further downstream from Seager's; William Todd built his sawmill still further downstream, below Cook's.

Dry Brook's most notable moment was when the naturalist John Burroughs launched his small boat from the creek for a journey down the East Branch of the Delaware River in the early 1880s, passing through what is now the Pepacton Reservoir.

Shandaken is a Dutch version of a Native American word for "place of the hemlocks."

Directions: Take Exit 19 off the New York State Thruway and drive west on Rt. 28 until you reach Arkville. From the west end of Arkville, continuing west on Rt. 28, cross over a small bridge spanning Dry Brook and immediately turn left onto Dry Brook Road. Follow Dry Brook Road southeast for approximately 9 miles. Just after you pass the last covered bridge, which will be on your left, you will reach a dead end at the trailhead for Seager Trail.

Hike the yellow-blazed Seager Trail, which parallels Dry Brook. Take note that although this is a state-maintained trail, it crosses private lands where hunting, fishing, and picnicking are not allowed. At roughly 0.8 mile you will come to the first waterfall, just down from a point where the trail comes close to the stream again and where hemlocks fill the forest.

You will come to the second fall a mere 0.05 mile further where a trail sign states that you are 0.9 mile from the trailhead.

To reach the third waterfall, continue along the Seager Trail for 0.1 mile. You will reach a point where the trail crosses Dry Brook. Fording the stream is necessary here, but easy unless you are negotiating the brook following snow melt or heavy rain. After crossing the stream, proceed steeply uphill, leaving the creek behind. After 0.2 mile you will hear the sound of Shandaken Brook off to your right in an area filled with hemlocks. Leave the trail and walk down 75 feet to the edge of the chasm.

Tompkins Falls

Location: West of Margaretville (Delaware County)

Accessibility: Near roadside; short, but steep 20-foot scramble down bank of stream

Degree of Difficulty: Easy to Moderate

Description: Tompkins Falls consists of a series of cascades formed on Barkaboom Stream, a small brook that rises to the west of Barkaboom Mountain and flows into the Pepacton Reservoir.

The falls, in descending order of height, are 3 feet, 6 feet, and 8 feet high and are contained in a ravine whose bedrock has been significantly sculptured by the stream. Look closely and you will see potholes and graceful contours where Barkaboom Stream has done its work.

On the south bank can be seen the foundation walls of an old factory.

History: Barkaboom Stream flows into the Pepacton Reservoir, which is the second largest body of water in the Catskills and one of six Catskill reservoirs impounding water to be transported down-state via huge underground aqueducts. The reservoir is 20 miles long and approximately 0.5 mile wide, created by damming the Pepacton River (the East Branch of the Delaware River) at Downsville, 1,280 feet above sea level.

It is said that Pepacton is the Indian name for "marriage of the waters."

In earlier geological times Barkaboom Stream flowed into a post-glacial lake that was created by a moraine (glacial deposit of debris) at Shinhopple, southwest of the present dam. After the natural barrier was worn down, the valley was emptied of water, with Barkaboom Stream flowing directly into the East Branch of the

Delaware River until the present reservoir was created.[1]

There have been a number of mills on Barkaboom Stream. In 1801, Eli Sears built a sawmill near the stream's confluence with the East Branch of the Delaware River. This was followed in 1848 by a mill built by Jenkins & Mekeel further up Barkaboom Stream, and in 1857, Andrew Hawver built his mill still further yet upstream.[2]

Directions: From Margaretville (junction of Rtes. 28 & 30N) proceed west on Rtes. 28 & 30 for 2.3 miles, and turn left onto an unmarked highway (called South Reservoir Road). Drive west along this road, paralleling the reservoir, for 8.4 miles. Turn left onto Barkaboom Road and drive uphill for 1.3 miles. The falls are on your right, at a roadside pull-off. A steep path leads down the embankment for 20 feet to the falls, which are on state land.

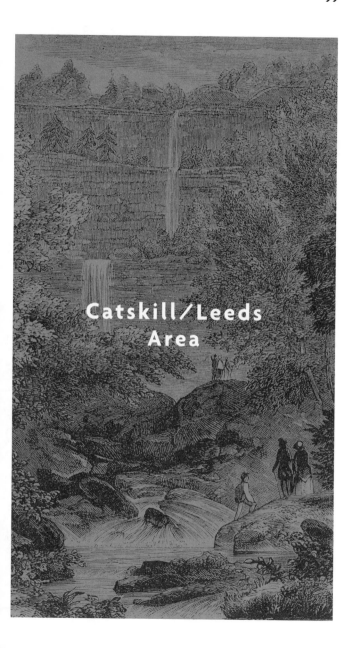

Catskill/Leeds
Area

Klein's Falls

Location: Near Catskill (Greene County)

Accessibility: Roadside

Description: Klein's Falls is formed on Kaaterskill Creek, a medium-sized stream that rises in the hills above Haines Falls and flows into Catskill Creek at Cauterskill.

The cascade is 12 feet high, very broad, and gently inclined. Debris, such as downed trees, tangles of branches, and brush can be found often near the shallows at the top of the falls—until the next deluge comes along to wash away the rubble.[1] An old, rusted metal bridge spans Kaaterskill Creek only a short distance above the cascade.

History: The first sawmill in the area of Klein's Falls was established by Van Bergen in 1690. Some time later a gristmill was built just below the falls.

In 1868 James Reid built the Reid Pistol Factory, which manufactured a barrel-less revolver known as the "knuckle duster."

Until recently, old foundations and ruins could be seen along the south bank just down from the falls. In 2003 the foundations were razed and the area was posted. If you look across the stream, however, you can still see surviving ruins along the river just east of a private residence.

Early pictures of the waterfall show a covered bridge spanning its top. According to J Van Vechten Vedder, "in 1815 a bridge was built across the stream, 'on or near the falls of Joseph Klein,' who had a mill at that place."[2] Covered bridges were popular in that era because bridges that were enclosed were better protected from the elements than those without roofs, thus ensuring their survival over a greater period of time. Early on, the bridge was called David Van Gelder's covered bridge.[3]

Kaaterskill Creek has also been spelled Cauterskill Creek in the past. *Kaats,* or Cats, is a prefix that was added to the Dutch word *kill* (meaning stream) to form the word Catskills. According to some writers the name was chosen because early settlers found the woods and streams to be replete with wildcats and panthers.

The nearby village of Catskill has a colorful history, having once served as the hideout for Legs Diamonds and Vincent Coll, notorious gangsters from the Roaring Twenties.

Directions: From I-87 (the NYS Thruway) get off at exit 21 for Catskill, turn left onto Rt. 23B, and drive east for 1.7 miles. Near the bottom of a long hill, turn right onto Rt. 9W and head south. You will immediately cross over Catskill Creek and come to a blinking traffic light where a high train trestle passes overhead. Turn right onto West Main Street and proceed west for 1.3 miles. At this point Rt. 30 enters from the left. Continue west on what is now Rt. 30 for another 0.5 mile and you will come to the falls, directly to your right.

Cauterskill Road (Rt. 47) crosses over Kaaterskill Creek at the top of the cascade and provides an opportunity to look down at the falls from the bridge.

Klein's Falls, when it was spanned by a covered bridge.

Old Covered Bridge at Cauterskill, Catskill Mountains.   T. H. Sachs, Publisher, Catskill, N.

Fall on High Falls Road Extension

Location: Near Kiskatom (Greene County)

Accessibility: Roadside

Description: This broad waterfall is formed on Kaaterskill Creek, a medium-sized stream that rises in the high reaches of Kaaterskill Clove and flows into Catskill Creek near Catskill. The fall is roughly 6 feet high, but fairly wide. Just above the waterfall is a 4-foot high dam impounding a small pond.

History: Kiskatom was once an Indian village. Its name means "place of thin-shelled hickory nuts."

Directions: From the NYS Thruway, get off at Exit 21, drive into Catskill, and continue southwest on Rt. 23A. From the point where Rt. 23A crosses over the NYS Thruway, continue driving west on Rt. 23A for another 2.3 miles.

If you are coming from the junction of Rtes. 32 and 23A between Catskill and Palenville, drive east on Rt. 23A for 1.3 miles.

Either way, when you come to High Falls Road Extension, turn onto it and drive southwest for 1.2 miles. When you arrive at a small bridge spanning Kaaterskill Creek, look to your right as you cross the bridge and you will see the fall just a short distance upstream.

Take note of the private homes along the stream's north bank and remain on the bridge. Enjoy the view, but do not disturb the privacy of any homeowner.

High Falls

Location: Near Kiskatom (Greene County)

Accessibility: Roadside

Description: High Falls, unfortunately, is on private lands and not accessible to the public, but from a small bridge spanning Kaaterskill Creek you can see the top of High Falls as it enters into a deep gorge "enclosed by rocky walls that rise precipitously 120 feet above the western edge and 80 feet above the eastern bank of the chasm."[1] The waterfall is impressive, but not as high as the name suggests, being a substantial, but hardly record-breaking 35-foot drop into the gorge below.[2]

Just a short distance upstream from the bridge is a pretty little, 3-foot-high cascade that stretches across the entire width of the stream.[3-4]

History: It is from the falls that the hamlet of High Falls and the road derive their names. High Falls has been known in the past by other names: Great Falls, according to a photograph in R. Lionel De Lisser's *Picturesque Catskills: Greene County;*[5] and Kaaterskill High Falls, according to Arthur G. Adams in his *The Hudson River*

High Falls is now inaccessible.

Guidebook. The "Kaaterskill" was added on to distinguish the falls from several others in the Catskills that were named High Falls.[6]

In 1837, Winthrop Laflin built a powder mill near the falls. Wooden barrels to contain the powder were supplied by a mill in Palenville. Not surprisingly, the production of volatile mixtures like gunpowder or fireworks posed significant health hazards for workers. In 1847 several men were killed and the building blown apart when gunpowder accidentally exploded. The mill was rebuilt and operated for a while longer, but production ceased in 1875 when there was another explosion.

Directions: Follow the directions given to the Fall on High Falls Road Extension. From there, drive southwest for 0.1 mile to High Falls Road. Turn left onto High Falls Road and drive south for 1.5 miles. At the junction with Nelson Hoff Road (which comes in on the right), continue left on High Falls Road and drive downhill for a little over 0.2 mile.

Pull off the road just before you cross over a bridge spanning Kaaterskill Creek. Walk out onto the bridge and look downstream. You will see the summit of High Falls at the point where the stream readies itself for an abrupt plunge into a deep gorge.

Remain on the bridge. The waterfall is on private land.

Look upstream and you will see another cascade 0.05 mile from the bridge. You can get a closer look at that cascade by driving up Mossy Hill Road, which parallels Kaaterskill Creek.

Roadside view of upper High Falls.

Falls at Austin Glen

Location: Catskill (Greene County)

Accessibility: There is a good view from the top of the Rt. 23 bridge, but the real problem is accessing the bridge. "No parking" signs extend in both directions from the bridge for hundreds of feet, which means you must walk 0.5 mile after parking the car in order to get to the bridge.

It is also possible to canoe upstream into Austin Glen from the confluence of the Catskill with the Hudson River, or from the Catskill's confluence with Kaaterskill Creek, but you must be a determined, highly competent kayaker or canoeist. Rapids, drops, and shallow waters must be negotiated, made all the more difficult because you will be paddling upstream.

Degree of Difficulty: Easy by foot, once you are at the bridge; difficult by canoe, unless you are an experienced white-water paddler willing to go against the current and to portage where necessary.

Description: The Falls at Austin Glen are formed on Catskill Creek, a fairly large stream that rises south of Middleburgh and flows into the Hudson River at Catskill. Catskill Creek constitutes the line of demarcation between the Catskills to the south, and the Helderbergs to the north.

Austin Glen is one of the most scenic, rugged gorges in the Catskills (or anywhere else in the northeast, for that matter), with towering cliffs, cascades, brisk rapids, and intriguing caves. The glen is described at some length in Clay Perry's caving classic, *Underground Empire*, written in the late 1940s as an attempt to codify the caves of New York State.[1]

According to Walter F. Burmeister, "Austin Glen is a gorge of some magnitude, however, its fascination is not found in immense proportions, but rather in a unique harmony between confining

narrows, wilderness-like rock-lined slopes, intricate ledge formations, impressive cliffs with densely wooded edges, and thundering
white water."[2]

The fall visible from the bridge is fairly broad, forming virtually a ruler's-edge line across most of the creek, as though it were a
man-made dam. The fall is roughly 6-8 feet high.

There are several smaller falls and cascades further downstream, deeper in the glen.[3]

History: Austin Glen contains its share of old ruins from past industrial efforts. Downstream from the fall is the foundation rubble of a
paper mill built around 1800 by Nathan Benjamin. When
Benjamin's mill burned down in 1807, Abner and Russell Austin, for
whom the glen is named, acquired the property and put up a new
mill in its place.

The old railroad bed of the Catskill Mountain Railroad, in operation until 1918, now forms an impressive walkway through the glen
following the east bank of Catskill Creek up to where the tracks
dead-end at the stream. There, bridge abutments are mute testimo-
ny to how the tracks then crossed over to the other side of the creek
and continued on.

Directions: From I-87 (the NYS Thruway) get off at Exit 21 for
Catskill/Cairo. Turn left onto Rt. 23B and drive east for 0.3 mile.
Turn right onto Rt. 23 and drive west for 0.7 mile, crossing over the
NYS Thruway in the process. When you come to the second bridge,
which spans Austin Glen, continue west until you reach Cauterskill
Road. Turn left at the light.

Park along Cauterskill Road and walk back along Rt. 23 for 0.5
mile to the bridge. You must remain alert and watch the traffic.
There are no sidewalks on the bridge, so you must wait until there
are no cars before venturing out on the bridge for a quick look. The
fall is visible from the south side of the bridge, but it is not possible
to see the fall when driving by because of the solid cement railing
on both sides of the bridge.

The falls and cascades further downstream cannot be seen
from the top of the bridge.

Directions by canoe or kayak: Put in at either the Catskill Creek's confluence with the Hudson River, or near where the Catskill Creek joins with Kaaterskill Creek. From the Hudson River it is an upstream paddle of approximately 4 miles; from Kaaterskill Creek it is a paddle of roughly 1 mile. Although the waters are fairly calm up to Catskill Creek's confluence with Kaaterskill Creek, they rapidly become agitated and turbulent as you paddle upstream and enter the glen. There are difficult drops and cascades to be negotiated, made all the more difficult because you are paddling upstream.

Fortunately, this trip doesn't require negotiating the worst section of Austin Glen, which is upstream from the waterfall, just below Mill Pond at Leeds.

To access Catskill Creek from the Hudson River, drive into the village of Catskill and follow Main Street east to its end. At the terminus of Main Street, turn left into Dutchman's Landing, where your kayak or canoe can be launched. Follow the Hudson River downstream for 0.1 mile and then turn right and proceed up Catskill Creek. Roughly one mile upstream from the Rt. 9W bridge, you will turn right onto Catskill Creek where Kaaterskill Creek comes in straight ahead.

You may find it possible to access Catskill Creek from other points along its length if you scout out possible launching sites and then get permission from the landowner.[4]

The wild gorge at Austin Glen.

Rip Van Winkle Falls

Location: Leeds (Greene County)

Accessibility: Distant view of top of falls from a public park

Description: This historically significant waterfall is formed on Catskill Creek, a large stream that rises 3 miles south of Middleburgh at Vlaie Pond and flows into the Hudson River at Catskill. The fall is approximately 15 feet high and has been known in the past as Austin Falls, Leeds Falls, and Great Falls, all fitting names since the fall is close to *Austin* Glen, found in *Leeds*, and (with some hyperbole) great in size.

At one time the waterfall was readily accessible to the public. Local youths would sit on its rocky ledges and swim in the waters below. A small power plant was built next to the fall years ago, however, and public access has been restricted ever since.

Gilfeather Park, less than 0.2 mile upstream from the fall, provides ready access to Catskill Creek. From Gilfeather Park, at a point where huge blocks of masonry face the river, you can look across at a number of tiny cascades and rapids along Catskill Creek. Downstream can be seen the faintly outlined top of Rip Van Winkle Falls, where a small, gray-colored building stands on the north bank.

History: Catskill Creek was heavily industrialized in the past in order to harness the power of its surging waters. According to *Guide to the Catskills,* "along one 27 mile stretch of Catskill Creek in 1836 there were 16 gristmills, 26 sawmills, 8 fulling mills, 7 carding machines, 1 woolen factory, an iron works, 2 paper mills, 1 brewery, and 10 tanneries."[1]

Leeds was the original site of Old Catskill, occupying the five great plains of the Indians. In 1711, a Mrs. Van Bergen and a man named Salisbury built a mill at the falls. Other mills quickly followed, and the name of the town, called Pasqoecq by Native Americans, became Mill Village in 1827. The villagers must have been fickle, however, for in that same year the name changed again, this time to Leeds in honor of Richard Hardwick, who was from Leeds, England.

By 1846, Harris and Harding had built a steam-powered woolen mill in Leeds and employed 150 people. Other businesses came and went over the next hundred years.[2]

The parking area at Gilfeather Park is on the site of two, former, large mills, and the area overlooked by the park is known to the locals as Marlboro Rocks.

The stone bridge that crosses Catskill Creek on the west side of town is the oldest in the state. Its eastern arches were constructed in 1760; its western arches in 1792. In 1936 major work had to be done on the bridge to preserve it. The bridge would have been demolished were it not for the efforts of local historian Jessie Van Vechten Vedder, who convinced New York State to dismantle the bridge, with each block of stone numbered, and rebuild it with its original integrity maintained.

Directions: From I-87 (the NYS Thruway) get off at Exit 21 for Catskill/Cairo, turn right onto Rt. 23B, and drive west for 1.2 miles into Leeds. In the center of town, turn left (south) onto Gilfeather Park Road, which is directly opposite the right-hand turn for Rt. 49. Follow Gilfeather Park Road to its end, a drive of less than 0.1 mile, going straight where the main back road veers to the left.

From the lookout at the terminus of Gilfeather Park, you can gaze downstream towards Rip Van Winkle Falls.

The area around the park, loaded with natural, fissured blocks of limestone, is well worth exploring in its own right.

Rip Van Winkle Falls.

Buttermilk Falls

Location: Near Leeds (Greene County)

Accessibility: Very short walk over moderately uneven terrain

Degree of Difficulty: Easy

Description: This scenic area contains three waterfalls, each one unique. The falls are formed on a tiny stream rising in the hills west of Green Lake and flowing into Catskill Creek at Leeds just a short distance west of the Leeds Bridge.

The first waterfall is 20 feet high and plunges over a straight ledge into a moderate-sized ravine. What's distinctive about the waterfall is that the stream comes in nearly perpendicular to the top of the fall, following a bed that is so linear as to make it seem almost artificially created.

A 6-foot, ledge waterfall is formed just downstream from the main fall.

The third waterfall is a large, 30-foot-high cascade formed at a point where the ravine opens into a deep glen with sheer bluffs along its east side. It is not advisable to bring little children or unleashed pets to visit this waterfall because of the high cliff face overlooking the cascade.

History: Buttermilk Falls is about as generic and common a name as a waterfall can have. Generally the name is a description of how the water is churned up at the base of the falls.

Directions: From I-87 (the NYS Thruway) get off at Exit 21 for Catskill/Cairo. Take Rt. 23B into Leeds, driving west for 1.2 miles. Turn right onto Rt. 49, which is Green Lake Road, and drive north for 2.2 miles. When you come to a fork in the road, bear to your left. This is Buttermilk Road. Go uphill for 0.4 mile. Look for a large pull-off on the left-hand side of the road with a yellow "arrow" next to it. You will see State Forest signs also. Park here.

A small path roughly 50 feet in length leads from the road to the top of the first fall. If you are visiting in early spring, you should be able to hear the falls from roadside. Just before you reach the top of the first cascade, there is a faint path that follows along the rim of the east bank. From this path, you can look back and get excellent views of the first fall.

The second fall is only 100 feet further downstream; you will find yourself looking down at it.

Continue along the east bank of the stream for another 100 feet, veering slightly left. There is no clearly defined path at this point. You will very quickly come to a view of the third cascade, where the stream suddenly drops 30 feet or more into a deep glen. Do not get close to the edge of the bank; there is a vertical drop of well over 50 feet.

One of several Buttermilk Falls to be found in the Catskills.

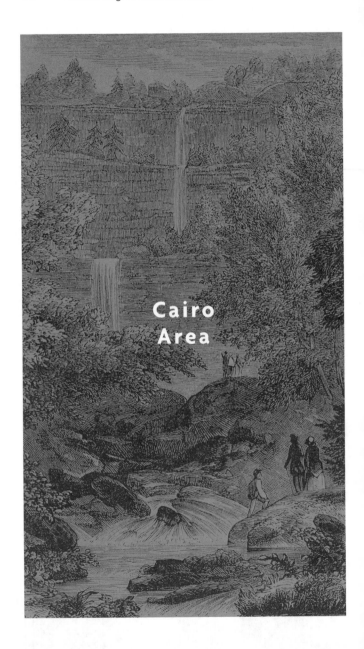

Cairo
Area

Falls at Woodstock Dam

Location: Near Cairo (Greene County)

Accessibility: Roadside

Description: There are several small falls near the Woodstock Dam that have formed on Catskill Creek, a large stream that rises south of Middleburgh and flows into the Hudson River by Catskill. In the same immediate area are two tributaries to Catskill Creek, both of which produce falls at their confluences. And finally, upstream from the falls is the Woodstock Dam, a 10-foot-high dam that has been breached for many years, but which still manages to produce its own pretty, though artificial waterfall.

None of the falls on Catskill Creek are individually of any great height, but when seen as a whole, they add up to a relief of about 30 feet. Combined with the falls on the two tributaries, the distinct impression is conveyed that this is an area dominated by falling waters.

The series of small, ledge-shaped waterfalls on Catskill Creek can be seen downstream from the bridge at the stream's confluence with the Platte Kill. According to Walter F. Burmeister, "in this area, the stream crosses a fault line, and the streambed consists of step-like ledges of reddish rock."[1] The gorge containing the falls has a rugged look to it; the fast moving waters of Catskill Creek have undercut the northern bank downstream from the bridge.

The Platte Kill, although comparatively small as a tributary, has also produced a cascade at the point where the stream flows into Catskill Creek slightly downstream from the bridge.

Just upstream from the bridge and directly across from the Woodstock Dam is a small, stair-like fall formed on yet another tributary to Catskill Creek

History: The bridge that spans Catskill Creek is part of an old highway system constructed in 1800 called the Woodstock & Durham Turnpike. Earlier bridges were built and replaced on at least three different occasions—twice because of being washed out by the rampaging Catskill Creek, and once because a drove of cattle overloaded the bridge. At least one of these earlier bridges was a covered bridge.

Years ago, the area associated with the falls supported a gristmill, sawmill, paper mill, woolen mill, and a distillery operated by Montgomery Stevens. The Woodstock Light & Power Company later operated a hydroelectric plant by the falls.[2]

Directions: From I-87 (the NYS Thruway) get off at Exit 21 for Catskill & Cairo. Drive west on Rt. 23 for roughly 8 miles until you reach Rt. 32 north by Cairo. Turn right onto Rt. 32 and drive northwest for 1.0 miles until you reach a bridge spanning Catskill Creek. The dam and falls are directly visible from the bridge. The problem is that "no parking" signs stretch out from the bridge to the north and south along both sides of the road, which means that in order to obtain a leisurely look, you must park beyond these signs and walk back to the bridge or have someone drop you off.

Multiple waterfalls can be seen near Woodstock Dam.

Shingle Kill Falls

Location: Purling (Greene County)

Accessibility: Permission from the Tumbling Falls Bed & Breakfast or the Shingle Kill Falls Bed & Breakfast will be necessary if you are not staying as guests at either inn.

Degree of Difficulty: Easy

Description: Shingle Kill Falls is formed on the Shingle Kill, a medium-sized stream that rises on the east shoulder of Blackhead Mountain and flows into Catskill Creek north of Cairo. The falls are 35 feet high, formed in red shale, and have been a featured attraction in Purling for centuries.[1-2]

Downstream from the waterfall, a small flume can be found, formed in the bedrock where the waters are forced through a narrow crevice and drop another 10 feet. A clock factory once stood nearby. In the same general area a small, 20-foot-high rivulet-type cascade descends from a tiny tributary on the west bank during the wet season.

There is a 5-foot-high fall upstream from the bridge above Shingle Kill Falls. A sawmill once used the stream for power at this location.

History: Shingle Kill Falls is located in an area known as the "Teutonic Catskills." The village of Purling acquired its name in 1895 from the purling (rippling) waters of the Shingle Kill. Previously the community had been known as Forge. Typical of the forges on the Shingle Kill was the iron forge built in 1788 by Enoch Hyde and Benjamin Hall of Litchfield, Connecticut. The iron was delivered by boats and mules from Ancram, Columbia County.

According to Tracy Lamanec, a seventh-generation owner of land at Shingle Kill Falls, a gristmill was built next to the falls around 1840, burned down in 1850, was rebuilt and then burned down again in 1892. The present mill at the top of the falls was erected in 1894 and used a waterwheel that was 28 feet in diameter and 6 feet wide. Just downstream from the gristmill and on the same side of the stream was a three-story wood turning mill that made grain cradles.

Directions: From I-87 (the NYS Thruway) get off at Exit 21 for Catskill and Cairo. Take Rt. 23 west, heading towards Cairo. When you come to Ross Ruland Road, which crosses Rt. 23 at a stoplight, continue straight ahead on Rt. 23 for another 0.8 mile, then turn left onto Silver Spur Road. Following Silver Spur Road southwest, be sure to stay on the lookout at 0.5 mile for a pretty, 6-foot-high water-fall in the woods to your right. Remain at roadside, however, for the waterfall is on private land. At 0.8 mile, Silver Spur Road crosses Rt. 32. Continue west for over another mile until you reach South Road. Turn right, and then immediately left onto Rt. 24. Within several hundred feet you will cross over the Shingle Kill just west of South Street. Shingle Kill Falls is directly downstream from the bridge spanning the Shingle Kill.

In the past you would access the waterfall by going to the Shingle Falls Grist Mill, located at roadside on the east bank, and paying a small fee to walk down to the base of the fall, or by stay-ing at the Tumbling Falls Bed & Breakfast on the west bank and leisurely exploring the fall and gorge from the inn. The Shingle Falls Grist Mill, however, has now become the Shingle Kill Falls Bed & Breakfast, which means that the fall is not directly accessible from either side without an arrangement being worked out with the man-agement of one of the inns.

Shingle Kill Falls.

Round Top
Area

Directions to Round Top: From I-87 (the NYS Thruway) get off at Exit 21 for Catskill & Cairo, and go west on Rt. 23 towards Cairo. When you come to Ross Ruland Road (which crosses Rt. 23 at a traffic light), continue straight on Rt. 23 for another 0.8 mile, and then turn left onto Silver Spur Road. Follow Silver Spur Road west for 2 miles into the village of Purling. Turn left onto South Road and drive south for 2 miles. When you get to Hearts Content Road (County Rt. 31), turn left and drive southeast for 0.7 mile. At Winter Clove Road turn right and proceed up to Round Top.

Glen Falls

Location: Round Top (near Cairo, Greene County)

Accessibility: 30-foot walk to platform overlook

Degree of Difficulty: Easy

Description: Glen Falls is formed on Kiskatom Brook, a small stream that rises near North Mountain and flows into Kaaterskill Creek near Kiskatom.

An observation platform provides an excellent view overlooking the top of Glen Falls as it drops into the gorge some 30 feet below. Bridal Veil Falls, the waterfall directly across from the lookout is formed on a tiny tributary to Kiskatom Brook and is roughly 25 feet in height. Together, Glen Falls and the smaller cascade on the adjacent tributary provide an unusual opportunity to see two waterfalls from one vantage point.

Glen Falls should not be confused with Glens Falls, a much larger and more heavily industrialized waterfall north of Albany in the upper Hudson Valley at the city of Glens Falls.

Glen Falls has been enjoyed by sightseers for over a century. A picture of the falls in *Picturesque Catskills: Greene County* shows a pavilion at the top of the falls and a house that stood much closer to the road than where the present Glen Falls House stands.[1]

Directions: Turn onto Winter Clove Road and drive south, going uphill, for 0.4 mile. Park to the side of the road when you reach Kiskatom Brook. Follow the wide pathway paralleling the north bank of the stream for 30-40 feet to a wooden observation platform. The buildings along the south bank of Kiskatom Brook by the falls comprise the Glen Falls House—a Catskill resort that provides lodging, meals, and a variety of activities. As a matter of courtesy, it would be proper to notify the management of the resort that you have come to look at the falls.

If you are a guest at the Glen Falls House, the management can direct you to 30-foot-high Icebox Falls, which is on the grounds of the resort and less than 0.5 mile away.

Glen Falls offers an unusual double waterfall.

Artist Falls

Location: Round Top (near Cairo, Greene County)

Accessibility: Short walk over uneven terrain

Degree of Difficulty: Easy

Description: Artist Falls is formed on Kiskatom Brook, a small stream that rises on the north slopes of North Mountain and flows into Kaaterskill Creek at Kiskatom.

The waterfall is 15 feet high, with a footbridge crossing over the stream at the top of the fall.[1]

History: The footbridge spanning the creek at the top of the waterfall was constructed in 1976 and dedicated to Alfred S. Clark. This is not the first footbridge, however, to span the fall. An earlier version was built out of logs and had rustic, wooden railings.

If you look carefully, you will find a faint, chiseled outline of Winter Clove Inn, in miniature, on the rock face near the base of the falls. Winter Clove Inn is a well-known Catskill resort and hiking Mecca, and a definite place to stay if you wish to linger in the Catskills for several days or weeks. It was built in 1830, and in 1838 H.B. Whitcomb opened up his farmhouse to guests, thus beginning a tradition that has endured for over 150 years.

The name Round Top came from the Indian word *Wa-wan-te-pe-kook,* meaning "round head place," apparently referring to the shape of the small mountain that looms over Purling and Cairo.

Directions: Turning south onto Winter Clove Road, drive uphill for 1.3 miles until you reach Winter Clove Inn. Notify management of your intended hike and ask permission to park in the inn's rear parking lot.

Walk back down the road past Winter Clove Inn. Several hundred feet northwest is Kiskatom Brook. Walk up the small hill next to the stream and you will reach a lovely, covered footbridge spanning the creek. The falls are directly below and can be accessed from a path leading to its base from the east bank, a short distance downstream from the footbridge.

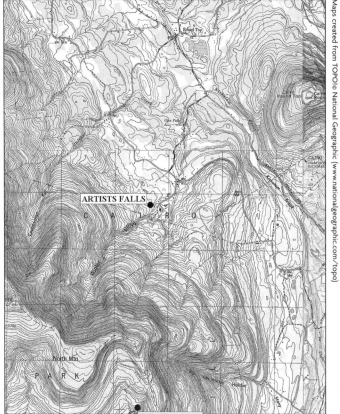

Maps created from TOPO!© National Geographic (www.nationalgeographic.com/topo)

Winter Clove Falls

Location: Round Top (near Cairo, Greene County)

Accessibility: 3.6-mile hike round-trip over uneven terrain with a moderate gain in elevation

Degree of Difficulty: Moderate to Difficult

Description: Winter Clove Falls is formed on Kiskatom Brook, a medium-sized stream that rises on the north shoulder of North Mountain and flows into Kaaterskill Creek at Kiskatom.

The falls consist of several drops and ledges totaling over 70 feet in height.

Approximately halfway along the hike up to Winter Clove Falls, just after the junction to a trail leading up to North Point, you will see several small cascades in a deep section of the gorge off to your right. Then, just before you begin a steep climb leading up to Winter Clove Falls, you will notice to your left a small fall formed on a tiny tributary to Kiskatom Brook.

Winter Clove Inn dates back to the 1800s.

History: Winter Clove was named by an early, post-Revolutionary War land surveyor who visited in the spring, only to find snow and ice in the clove when the valley below was ablaze with sunshine and warmth.

Directions: Turning south onto Winter Clove Road, drive uphill for 1.3 miles until you reach Winter Clove Inn. Notify management of your intended hike and ask permission to park in the inn's rear parking lot. From Winter Clove Inn follow the directions to Artist Falls (see previous hike). From Artist Falls follow the dirt road south, paralleling the east bank of Kiskatom Brook, for over 0.2 mile. Within a short length of time you will pass by a barn on your right and then, after proceeding up a steep hill, you will reach a large, two-door garage. Next to the garage is the red-blazed trail leading to Winter Clove Falls. From this point, the distance to the falls is approximately 1.5 miles.

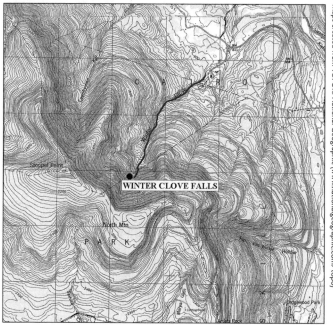

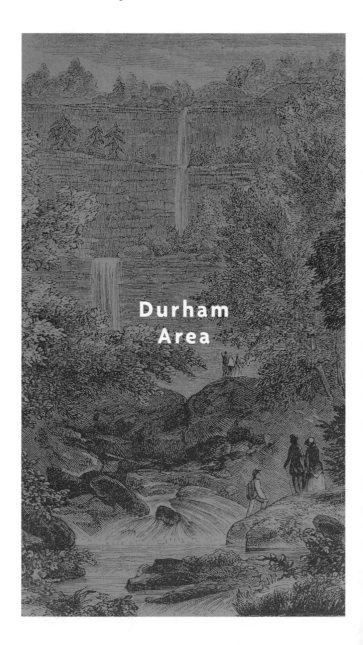

Durham
Area

Falls in South Durham

Location: South Durham (Greene County)

Accessibility: Roadside

Description: This small, charming waterfall is formed on a tiny tributary to Bowery Creek. The cascade is 10 feet high, falling into a narrow ravine. Remnants of an old stone wall remain at the top of the fall, and an old foundation can be seen along the south bank just downstream from the cascade.

Directions: From I-87 (the NYS Thruway) get off at Exit 21 for Catskill & Cairo, and proceed west on Rt. 23 for roughly 8.5 miles. Where Rtes. 23 & 145 divide, continue west on Rt. 23. After you have driven 4.7 miles from the junction of Rtes. 23 & 145, you will see a sign on your right for South Durham. Turn right onto Old State Rt. 23 and follow the road for about 0.6 mile. You will see the fall on your left where a tiny pull-off allows you to park at the top of the bank. If you come to Morrison Road on your right, then you have gone too far.

Take note of posted signs and remain at roadside, where good views are easily obtained.

Fall in East Durham

Location: East Durham (Greene County)

Accessibility: Roadside

Description: This waterfall is formed on Thorp Creek, a medium-sized stream that rises at Lookout Point near East Windham and merges with the Catskill Creek east of East Durham.

The fall is 25 feet high and located directly under a bridge spanning Thorp Creek. According to J. Van Vechten Vedder, "The gorge at East Durham is 50 feet deep, and the water near the grist-mill is very deep."[1]

Indications of past industrial days abound at the fall. Ruins can be seen at the bottom of the gorge, and a section of old dam is visible at the top of the waterfall. Slightly upstream from the fall, along the south bank, can be seen a wall of stone blocks.[2]

History: Thorp Creek has also been known as Fall Creek, and for very good reason. "It has in many places a rocky bed, and numerous falls, from 10 to 40 feet high." The stream was named after Captain Aaron Thorp who operated a sawmill nearby in 1790.

East Durham is informally known as the "Irish Alps," a name that arose after the area began attracting large numbers of Irish immigrants in the 1880s.

Directions: From I-87 (the NYS Thruway) get off at Exit 21 for Catskill & Cairo, and drive west on Rt. 23 for roughly 8.5 miles. Northwest of Cairo, where Rtes. 23 & 145 divide, turn right onto Rt. 145 and proceed northwest for 6.5 miles. When you reach East Durham, turn right onto Stone Bridge Road Ext. at the center of town. Immediately you will cross over Thorp Creek. Park to the side of the road. The top of the fall is visible from the bridge.

The sawmill is gone, but the ruins remain.

Falls at Zoom Flume

Location: Near East Durham (Greene County)

Accessibility: Commercial attraction; entrance fee required

Degree of Difficulty: Easy

Description: There are several falls that have formed on a medium-sized tributary to the Cornwallville Creek/Thorp Creek system in an area called Shady Glen. The falls are now contained in a major Catskills tourist attraction known as Zoom Flume. The natural gorge and waterfalls have been incorporated tastefully into the artificial world of the park's pools and slides, producing a setting that is relatively inoffensive to nature purists. Zoom Flume offers a unique opportunity to relax, frolic, and safely enjoy water activities, including a 300-foot water chute, while surrounded by natural waterfalls. The park is open to the public from late June to Labor Day.[1]

History: The two falls, known historically as Rumble-Tumble and Shimmering Falls, are both located within the park's perimeter and are visible from the restaurant's stairway, the cable bridge that crosses the gorge just above the falls, and from several walkways and platforms that are strategically placed within the interior of the gorge.

Shady Glen is a thickly wooded gorge about one-half mile long with steep rocks on one side and high banks on the other. The glen was the site of a wood-turning mill at one time.[2-3]

Directions: From Exit 21 of the NYS Thruway (I-87), proceed west on Rt. 23 for roughly 8.5 miles. At the point where Rtes. 23 & 145 converge near Cairo, turn right onto Rt. 145 and proceed northwest for 6.5 miles to East Durham. Continue northwest on Rt. 145 for roughly 1.3 miles from the third blinking traffic light in East

Durham; you will see signs pointing the way to Zoom Flume. Turn left onto Stone Bridge Road and drive west for 1.6 miles, then turn right onto Shady Glen Road. The park will be directly on your right.

Shimmering Falls is now part of Zoom Flume.

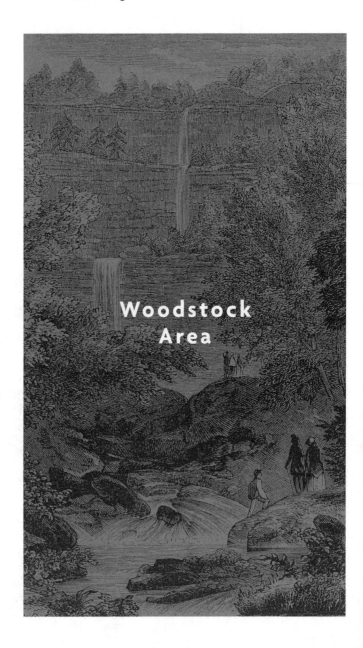

Woodstock
Area

Falls on Sawkill

Location: Woodstock (Ulster County)

Accessibility: Roadside

Description: This series of small falls is formed on the Sawkill, a medium-sized stream that rises at Echo Lake north of Overlook Mountain and whose waters are joined by a small creek coming down from Cooper Lake northwest of Woodstock. The Sawkill ultimately enters Esopus Creek north of Kingston.

The falls consist of a series of 2 to 3-foot ledge cascades and can be viewed quite nicely from the top of the Rt. 375 bridge.[1]

Woodstock, of course, will always be associated with the first of the mega rock concerts. Much earlier, however, Woodstock was already known as a cultural and countercultural center. In the early 1900s the town became the center of the Art Students League of New York and was heavily influenced by the American Bohemian movement. Not surprisingly, the town ended up divided between the old guard and the irreverent young. Even the Sawkill was not spared. According to Alf Evers, in *The Catskills: From Wilderness to Woodstock,* "Righteous citizens skulked among the bushes along the Sawkill which flowed through Woodstock, hoping to detect instances of 'nude bathing.'"[2]

Interestingly, the Sawkill, which presently rises at Echo Lake, at one time formed the headwaters of the Beaverkill, flowing southwest into Esopus Creek at Mount Tremper. Through an act of what geologists call "stream piracy," the Sawkill was captured prior to the last glacial period by another stream and diverted to its present course, which is a fairly straight run down to the Hudson River.

Robert Livingston built the first sawmill in the area; J. Montrose, the first gristmill. Soon after, a number of other sawmills and gristmills followed, and undoubtedly it was the plethora of sawmills that gave the creek its name.

According to a historical marker by the bridge at the falls, a carding mill owned by Joshua Nash operated at this site in the early 1800s.

Directions: From I-87 (the NYS Thruway) get off at Exit 20 for Saugerties. Go west on Rt. 212 until you reach Woodstock. Just as you approach the edge of the village, turn left onto Rt. 375. You will immediately cross over the Sawkill. Turn right at the end of the bridge and park off to the side on Millstream Road. Walk back onto the bridge and you will be afforded excellent views of the cascades upstream.

Risley Falls was once a favorite swimming hole in Woodstock.

Falls on Tannery Brook

Location: Woodstock (Ulster County)

Accessibility: Roadside

Description: Two small falls can be found on Tannery Brook, a small creek that enters the Sawkill at Woodstock. Both waterfalls are located in the village of Woodstock, a well-known artists' colony and namesake of the historic Woodstock music festival that so captured the mood of the late 1960s.[1-2]

It would seem that the brook was named for the multitude of tanneries that inhabited the stream. One of the earliest tanneries, built in 1875, was located near the intersection of Tannery Brook Road and Tinker Street.

Falls #1. The first waterfall is 8-10 feet in height and formed in a small ravine. The fall rushes over a medium-sized ledge, with houses and businesses on both sides of the ravine preventing any close-up views. A small dam can be seen just upstream from the fall, before the Rt. 212 bridge.

This area was the site of a tannery that endured from 1830 to 1870. According to a nearby historical marker, the hemlock bark used by the tanneries was shipped up the Hudson River from nearby Kingston.

Falls #2. The second waterfall consists of a series of three, 2-foot-high cascades that are quite visible from roadside.

Directions: From I-87 (the NYS Thruway) get off at Exit 20 for Saugerties. Proceed west on Rt. 212, going through the hamlet of Centerville in the process, until you reach the village of Woodstock. In the middle of Woodstock, Rt. 212 turns abruptly left. Right after this bend, you will come to a tiny bridge that crosses Tannery Brook.

Before crossing the stream, turn left onto Tannery Brook Rd. and park in a medium-sized parking lot just down the lane to your left.

You can also approach these cascades by turning left onto Rt. 375 from Rt. 212 (just as you would to see the falls on the Sawkill), and then immediately turning right onto Millstream Road. Drive west for 0.4 mile, paralleling the Sawkill, and then turn right onto Tannery Brook Road. Drive for less than 0.2 mile and there will be several areas where you can park.

Falls #1: Walk over to the west side of Tannery Brook Rd. by Sweetheart Gallery, and look upstream. From here you will be able to see the fall and the small dam just above the fall.

It is also possible to see the fall and dam from the top of the Rt. 212 bridge, but it is a limited view since you are looking downstream directly over the top of the falls.

To Falls #2: Continue walking down Tannery Brook Rd. for 0.1 mile and veer right, instead of going straight onto Pine Grove St. Immediately, you will walk onto a small bridge overlooking Tannery Brook. There are several small cascades that can be seen from the bridge. If you continue walking south for another 0.05 mile, you will come to a second bridge, this time spanning the Sawkill. From here can be seen some tiny cascades. This bridge is called Sully's Bridge, named after Dan Sully, an entertainer-turned-sawmill-owner. At one time the cascades upstream from the bridge were a popular swimming hole, but swimming there is now discouraged by the town.

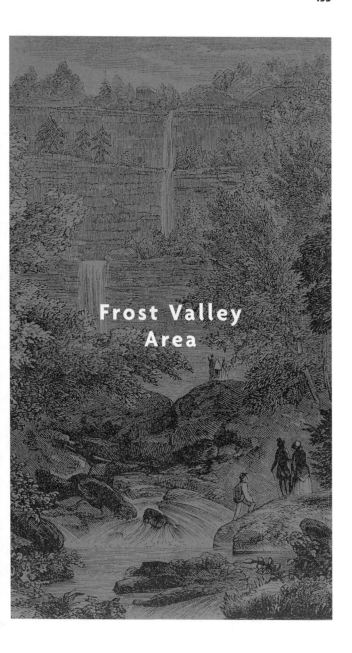

Frost Valley
Area

High Falls

Location: Frost Valley (Ulster County)

Accessibility: Short walk to fall from tiny parking area; access is restricted to registered guests in residence at the Frost Valley YMCA, organized prearranged marketing tours, and members of the Frost Valley natural resource programs.

Degree of Difficulty: Easy

Description: High Falls is formed on High Falls Brook, a small stream that rises south of Doubletop Mountain and flows into the West Branch of the Neversink River. The waterfall is over 40 feet high, consisting of a fairly straight plunge over the top onto the rocks below.[1] A wooden platform across from the base of the fall provides a convenient view of the waterfall.

Slightly upstream is a 10-foot waterfall.

History: High Falls is located on the 6,000-acre grounds of the Frost Valley YMCA. The main campus is at 2000 Frost Valley Road; the Straus Center for Adult Education is on 21 Straus Lane. The campus is visited annually by over 30,000 guests, with High Falls one of its main natural attractions.

Frost Valley was named for the unusually cold winters experienced there by early settlers.

Directions: From I-87 (the NYS Thruway) get off at Exit 19 for Kingston and Rhinecliff Bridge, and proceed west on Rt. 28. When you come to the hamlet of Big Indian, which is several miles west of Shandaken (junction of Rtes. 23 & 42), turn left onto Rt. 47. Drive up over the shoulder of Slide Mountain and then down the other side. Along the way, near the top of the mountain, you will pass the hiking trail to Giant Ledge. Just past Winooski Lake is the trailhead to Slide Mountain. The Frost Valley YMCA is to your right approximately 14 miles from Rt. 28. This is where you will need to report in order to access High Falls. To register or to obtain more information: write to Frost Valley YMCA, 2000 Frost Valley Road, Claryville, NY 12725-5221; call (845) 985-2291; or e-mail at www.frostvalley.org

Round Pond Falls

Location: Frost Valley (Ulster County)

Accessibility: Roadside

Description: This two-tiered waterfall is formed on a small creek that issues from Round Pond and flows into the West Branch of the Neversink River. The falls are approximately 20 feet high.

Directions: From I-87 (the NYS Thruway) get off at Exit 19 for Kingston and proceed west on Rt. 28 until you reach the hamlet of Big Indian. Turn left onto Rt. 47 and drive south for roughly 14 miles, going over the mountain range and down the other side. When you see the Frost Valley YMCA on your right, continue driving south for another 5.3 miles. (Along the way you will cross over tiny High Falls Brook, on which High Falls can be found upstream.) You will see a waterfall to your right, quite visible from roadside where the road curves to the left. A pull-off next to the fall allows you to park and enjoy the scenery, which includes the West Branch of the Neversink River to your left.

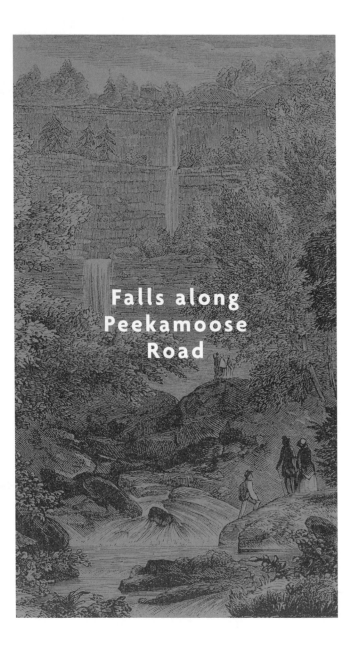

Falls along
Peekamoose
Road

Six Unnamed Falls and Buttermilk Falls

Location: Between West Shokan and Sundown (Ulster County)

Accessibility: Roadside

Description: Peekamoose Road, connecting West Shokan (a tiny hamlet near the Ashokan Reservoir) with Sundown (an even tinier hamlet formed at the confluence of Sundown Creek and Rondout Creek), could be justifiably called "The Waterfall Road," for it takes you past more than half a dozen roadside waterfalls within a span of two miles. In doing so, you will go up one side of a mountain, past a mountain lake, and down the other side of the mountain through a deep gorge formed between Peekamoose Mountain (3,843 ft.) to the north and Samson Mountain (2,812 ft.) and Bangle Hill (2,350 ft.) to the south.

Four large waterfalls can be seen along the west escarpment, and another three across the river along the east escarpment. All except one are contained in the stupendous gorge carved out by Rondout Creek. During periods of exceptionally heavy rainfall or snowmelt, other waterfalls may appear.[1-3]

History: R. Lionel De Lisser had this to say about Peekamoose Gorge:

> Further down the stream the Rondout enters Peekamoose Gorge, and flows through it for nearly a mile. On each side rise the perpendicular or overhanging rocks to the height of over one hundred feet, the top clad with stately trees, the shadow of whose far-reaching branches add to the gloom and mystery of the depths below. Through this cañon rushes the Rondout Creek, leaping over high bowlders and rocks that in the course of time have fallen from the ledges above.[4]

The pass, now traversed by Peekamoose Road, was not always so friendly and benign. During the last glacial period a huge wall of ice temporarily blocked the Esopus Creek from draining into the Hudson Valley. Water was diverted through Peekamoose Gorge and raced down the ravine in a mighty torrent. The tremendous force of this ancient stream carved out huge potholes and heavy glacial beds that are visible today in the notch.

In colonial days when war broke out with the Dutch, Native American warriors used the gulf as a route to swoop down on villagers below. The name Rondout Creek came from a fort (called a "redoubt") that was built in 1660 near the mouth of the stream.[5]

Earlier, Peekamoose Road was known as Gulf Road, which seems more fitting than its present, less descriptive name.

A sawmill once stood at the headwaters of the Rondout. Undoubtedly the mill was located in the area now occupied by several houses.

Directions: The drive begins at the junction of Rtes. 28A & 42 near West Shokan. To get there, get off the NYS Thruway (I-87) at Exit 19 for Kingston and drive west on Rt. 28 for about 16 miles. At Boiceville turn south (left) onto Rt. 28A and drive around the western perimeter of the Ashokan Reservoir for 3 miles. When you get to Rt. 42 at West Shokan, set your odometer reading to 0.0 and begin driving southwest on Rt. 42.

Take note that unless you set your odometer at the start of the trip, you will most likely miss some of the waterfalls, which may be difficult to spot unless you know approximately where to look. Be aware that mileage readings are approximations and may vary slightly from one vehicle to the next.

At 4.0 miles from the junction of Rtes. 28A & 42 as you begin the long climb up the mountain, you will pass by the trailhead parking on your right for Kanape Brook, a trail that parallels a fast-moving stream for part of its length and eventually leads to the top of Ashokan High Point.

At 6.0 miles you will pass by the first waterfall, which is on your right and easy to miss because it is recessed from roadside. If you drive by and don't spot it, turn around when you get to the north end of Peekamoose Lake and drive back, going south for 0.7 mile.

The waterfall is on posted land, but by pulling over to the side of the road and standing next to the creek, you can see it through the trees as it looms over 60 feet high in the distance. When sufficient water is flowing, the waterfall is a wide sheet of water falling over a smooth cliff face. Bear in mind that this waterfall and many of the ones to follow are best seen in the early spring when the trees are bare of leaves and the streams are tumbling into the gorge at maximum flow.

At 6.7 miles you will reach the north end of Peekamoose Lake, which is a narrow body of water some 0.4 mile in length that forms the headwaters of Rondout Creek.

The waters emanating from Peekamoose Lake, captured at an elevation of 1,677 feet above the Hudson River, join forces with the many streams coming into Peekamoose Gorge to form Rondout Creek. From Peekamoose Gorge, Rondout Creek races on for 40 miles further to the Rondout Reservoir. At the reservoir, the waters are either sent again along their way towards the Hudson River, or siphoned off through huge underground aqueducts for downstate consumption.

At 7.1 miles you will arrive at the south end of Peekamoose Lake. Slow down. If you look back, you will see a tiny dam-created fall at the end of the lake. You will also notice a stream that runs downhill from the west and joins the creek emanating from the lake. Look closely and you will see a pretty cascade on this upper stream, next to a private residence.

From this point you will begin your descent into the gorge created eons ago by Rondout Creek.

At 7.8 miles you will come to an unobstructed view from roadside of a large, hulking 40-foot waterfall to your right. Take note, however, that the fall is on posted land, and that even though there is a pull-off directly in front of the waterfall, the signs are very clear about "no parking." Drive south for another 50-100 feet and park where the land is state-owned. From here you can walk back to the waterfall for a leisurely view from roadside without fear of offending, but you must remain on the road.

At 7.9 miles, approximately where you may have parked in order to walk back to view the 40-foot waterfall, look to the east across to the other side of Rondout Creek and you should see off in the woods a tall, slender, high-dropping waterfall.

At **8.1** miles, looking east across to the opposite side of Rondout Creek, you will see another waterfall on your left. This waterfall also forms quite high up and drops over ledges as it approaches the bottom near Rondout Creek.

At **8.3** miles you will come to a roadside waterfall directly to your right. Park in the tiny pull-off on your left. This waterfall consists of a series of cascades, one after the other, dropping for a total height of over 70 feet. A little path on the left side of the stream goes up for a short distance, but only to near the base of the fall. The fall is best viewed from roadside.

At **8.5** miles look again to your left (eastward) and you will see yet another high-forming waterfall coming in on the opposite side of Rondout Creek. Be patient if you don't spot it immediately. All of the falls across Rondout Creek along the east escarpment can be difficult to find, even under the best of conditions and even when you know approximately where to look.

Continue southwest on Peekamoose Road for 0.5 mile more and pull into a parking area on your right at 9.0 miles, just north of a fall up ahead. A trail paralleling the road leads from the parking area to the base of Buttermilk Falls, a 40-foot-high waterfall formed on a small stream that rises south of Rocky Mountain. Buttermilk Falls is the waterfall that people generally go to see in this gorge. It is impressive, accessible at roadside, and possesses a mostly reliable flow of water. More so than the other high falls in the gorge, Buttermilk has carved out a rugged gully at the top of the escarpment, forming a tiny chasm directly at the top of the fall. Upstream from the chasm are several pretty cascades including a 5-footer, an elongated 10-foot cascade, and a nearly vertical 15-foot drop.

If you continue further along Peekamoose Road for another 1.0 mile, you will reach the trailhead for Peekamoose Mountain on your right, leading up to its main destination, Reconnoiter Rock (2,900 feet).

Alternate Directions: If you are approaching from the southeast, coming up Rt. 209 from Ellenville, turn northwest onto Rt. 55 at Napanoch and proceed toward the Rondout Reservoir. As you near the reservoir, turn right onto Rt. 55A and continue traveling north-west almost to the western perimeter of the reservoir. Then turn right onto Rt. 153 and travel northeast. When you reach the tiny hamlet of Sundown, turn left after crossing over a bridge onto Peekamoose Road and drive northeast for another 4 miles. You will see Buttermilk Falls on your left. From this starting point, the water-falls can be seen in the reverse of the order given above.

Along
Route 17

Rt. 17, also known as "the Quickway," provides
ready access to several falls in the southwestern
Catskills that are difficult to access from the north.

146

Fall in Ferndale

Location: Ferndale (Sullivan County)

Accessibility: Roadside

Description: This cascade is formed on Mongaup River, a large stream that rises west of the Neversink Reservoir and flows into the Delaware River northwest of Port Jervis. The cascade is a 6-foot drop contained in an area of interesting bedrock.

History: At one time the Fall in Ferndale was topped by a large dam that impounded the stream above the waterfall, diverting water through a large pipe to a gristmill on the west bank.[1]

Ferndale is named for the many ferns that once grew in the "dale," a quaint English word meaning "valley."

Directions: Driving northwest from Monticello along Rt. 17, get off at Exit 101 for Ferndale and Swan Lake. Immediately turn right and drive 0.2 mile. Turn right onto Rt. 71 and proceed south for 0.4 mile. Look for The Inn by the Falls, which will be to your left. The fall can be seen from the parking area next to the inn.

The Inn by the Falls is a seasonal restaurant, closed during the winter. In-season it is well worth taking advantage of the extraordinary opportunity to enjoy a meal while seated next to the large window overlooking this energetic waterfall while.

The fall in Ferndale during its industrial days.

Fall in Parksville

Location: Parksville (Sullivan County)

Accessibility: Roadside

Description: This waterfall is formed on a small stream that rises from branches issuing out of Lily Pond and Cranberry Pond, and flows into the Little Beaverkill at Parksville.

The fall is 10 feet in height, plunging over a streambed that is uniquely composed of brown-colored rock.

Directions: Drive north on Rt. 17 roughly 6 miles from Ferndale and get off at Exit 98 for Parksville, turning right when you come to the traffic light. Head northeast, going uphill for 0.2 mile, and then turn left onto West Lily Pond Road. Almost immediately the road crosses over a stream. Pull over next to the bridge and you will be afforded excellent views of the fall, which is directly upstream.

Another pretty roadside waterfall.

Falls on Tributary to Willowemoc Creek

Location: Near Parksville (Sullivan County)

Accessibility: 0.8-mile hike round-trip

Degree of difficulty: Moderate

Description: There are several waterfalls formed on a tributary to Willowemoc Creek, a medium-sized stream that rises in the hills northeast of Willowemoc and flows into the Little Beaverkill at Livingston Manor.

Maps created from TOPO!© National Geographic (www.nationalgeographic.com/topo)

Fall #1 is a 10-foot-high cascade formed out of a series of ledges and falling into a pretty glen. Fall # 2 is a 4-foot-high cascade tumbling down the stream next to several large slabs of rock. Fall # 3 consists of a 15-foot-high plunge fall, dropping into an amphitheater of rock.[1]

Directions: From Rt. 17 get off at Exit 98 for Parksville. Drive uphill on Cooley Road (Rt. 84/85) and proceed northeast for 4.9 miles. Turn left onto Anderson Road (a dirt road) and drive north for 0.3 mile. Turn right onto Conklin Hill Road and proceed downhill, going north for 1.0 mile until you come to a covered bridge that spans Willowemoc Creek. Park to your right before the bridge.

Cross over the stream directly behind the parking area, and follow a faint, unmarked trail that parallels the east bank of the creek upstream. The first fall is encountered after you have gone 0.2 mile. The second, fairly small fall is found directly around the bend above the first fall. Waterfall # 3, the largest and most impressive of the three, is less than 0.2 mile further upstream.

Russell Brook Falls

Location: Near Butternut Grove (Delaware County)

Accessibility: Less than 0.1-mile walk round-trip

Degree of Difficulty: Easy

Description: Russell Brook Falls is formed on Russell Brook, a small stream that rises in the hills north of Cooks Falls and flows into the Beaverkill at Butternut Grove.

The waterfall is roughly 30 feet high and contained in a scenic glen. Just downstream from the fall can be seen the stone abutments of a bridge that once spanned the creek. If you stand next to the bridge abutment along the west side of the creek, you can look across Russell Brook and see the outline of where the road to the bridge once continued, paralleling the stream.[1-2]

At the top of the fall is a breached dam. Further upstream are the stone foundations of a second dam, also breached, where the date 1895 has been carved into one of its huge blocks. Below this upper dam is an elongated, 10-foot-high cascade.

History: According to Leslie C. Wood, a small waterfall that once posed a natural barrier to river traffic on the Beaverkill at Buttermilk Grove was blasted to bits in order to increase the river's range of navigability. An "up and down" sawmill once operated on Russell Brook.[3]

Directions: Drive west along Rt. 17 and get off at Exit 93 for Cooks Falls, approximately 11 miles from Livingston Manor. At the end of the exit ramp, turn left and drive west for 0.1 mile to Buttermilk Grove. Turn right onto Russell Brook Road and drive northeast for 3.8 miles. At 0.8 mile you will observe a sign stating that the road is seasonal, which means that this trek should not be undertaken during the winter months when snow or ice may cover the road. At

3.8 miles turn into the trailhead parking on your left. If you go too far, you will reach Morton Road on your right.

Follow an old abandoned road in front of the parking area. The road leads downhill to the stream. In less than 0.05 mile you will cross over Russell Brook when you come to a tiny bridge. Then follow a path to your right that leads up to the falls, clearly visible upstream. The path quickly leads to an old bridge abutment, and then to the base of the fall.

A slightly higher path takes you to the midsection of the fall, where excellent views can be obtained. Exercise caution. This path is fairly broad, but there are sharp drops to your right.

On your return drive along Russell Brook Road, pull over at 2.8 miles, just before reaching the Russell Brook Campsite. Look over to your right, across Russell Brook to the opposite bank, where an enormous, abandoned waterwheel can be seen jutting out from a cement enclosure that at one time flowed with water.

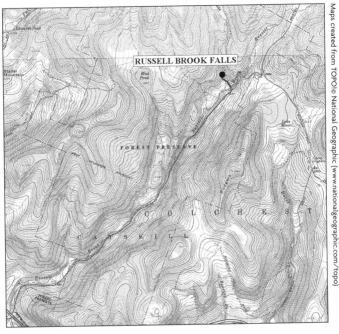

Potholes are often associated with waterfalls. How they come to form is an example of poetry in motion:

Poem Number Seven

Where water flows
And so speeds up
It finally slows
To fill a cup

Of stone scooped out
By water's spin.
As through a spout
It enters in.

Then overflows
So filling up
Each saucer there
Of earthenware.

From *Forty Falls*
© 2003 Chuck Gibson

Section II

The Shawangunks or "Gunks," as they are more informally called, are the northern continuation of the Kittatinny Ridge of New Jersey and the Blue Ridge of Pennsylvania—both of which are upper sections of the Appalachian Range. Although the Gunks are in close proximity to the Catskills, the two mountain regions have little in common. The Shawangunks were formed out of an entirely different kind of rock and raised up in a mountain building process totally different from that of the Catskills.

The Shawangunks are made of an extremely durable rock called Shawangunk conglomerate, which is composed of minute grains and coarse particles that were cemented together under intense heat and pressure within the earth some 400 million years ago. Underlying the conglomerate bed is a layer of Martindale shale, which is a slightly older rock created 70 million years earlier. When intense pressures inside the earth raised the Gunks, buckling and tilting the bedrock in the process, sections of the underlying Martindale shale were exposed as well. Because Martindale shale erodes more readily, it has undercut the more durable Shawangunk conglomerate in places, causing huge blocks of conglomerate to break off in clean fracture lines, leaving behind vertical cliff faces of very tough rock. This is what makes the Gunks so attractive to rock climbers, who consider the area to be the best in the eastern United States for rock climbing.

Waterfalls of the Shawangunks

The Shawangunks contain a number of diverse and unique waterfalls. The most impressive of these falls are found in the northern Shawangunks—an area some 20 miles long and 6 miles across at its widest, extending from Cragsmoor to Rosendale. This area is delineated to the west by Rondout Creek, and to the east by the Wallkill River. Both streams converge north of the Shawangunks near Lefever Falls to join with the Hudson River at Kingston.

The glaciers that retreated over 10,000 years ago had a small, but significant effect on waterfall formation in the Gunks. The glaciers sharpened many of the cliffs, accentuating their heights and making for more dramatic waterfall plunges. These glaciers also deepened the bedrock along fault lines and carried away huge piles of rock debris, allowing bigger lakes to form and more water to be released along streambeds to create the impressive waterfalls that you see today.

This section includes waterfalls in the areas surrounding the Gunks as well, where many waterfalls can be visited that are either roadside or require minimum effort to reach.

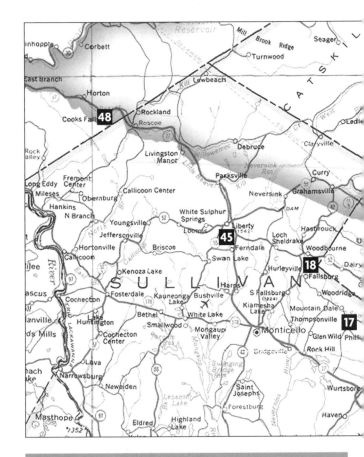

Waterfalls of the Shawangunks

Minnewaska State Park
1. Awosting Falls
2. Sheldon Falls
3. Falls on Sanders Kill
4. Stony Kill Falls
5. Rainbow Falls
6. Split Rock Falls

Area along Route 209
7. High Falls
8. Falls on Lower Coxing Kill
9. Falls on Tributary to Coxing Kill
10. Dashville Falls

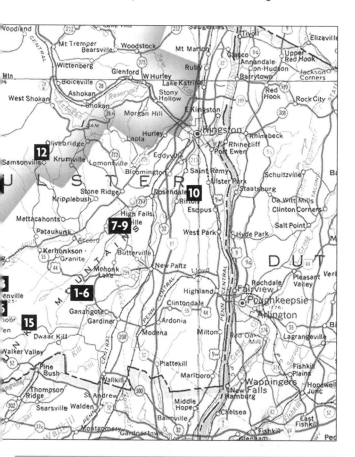

Map Key

Napanoch/Wawarsing Area
11. Vernooy Kill Falls
12. Falls on Mettacahonts Creek
13. Napanoch Falls
14. Honk Falls

Ellenville Area
15. Verkeerder Kill Falls
16. Nevele Falls

17. Tomsco Falls Park
18. Cascades at Fallsburg

Numbers 45 and 48
are keyed on page viii.

Note: shaded area indicates
boundaries of the Catskill Park.

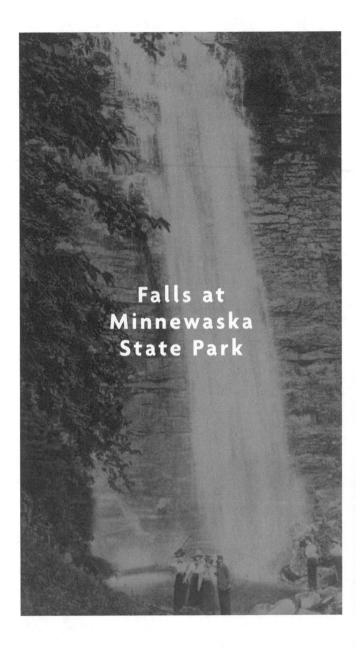

Falls at
Minnewaska
State Park

Minnewaska State Park encompasses over 12,000 acres of breathtakingly beautiful landscape, including Lake Awosting, Lake Minnewaska, and a number of high waterfalls. The park's 25 miles of hiking trails and 27 miles of carriage roads encourage countless hours of exploration over a vast expanse of rugged terrain.

Lake Minnewaska, once known as Coxing Pond, is the centerpiece of the park and starting point for hikers making their way to Millbrook Mountain, Gertrude's Nose, Castle Point, Awosting Falls, Sheldon Falls, Rainbow Falls, and Stony Kill Falls. Unlike Lake Awosting, which requires a 3-mile hike to reach, Lake Minnewaska is readily accessible by anyone with an automobile.

At an elevation of 1,652 feet, Lake Minnewaska is a product of the last ice age. Cliffs rise up as high as 145 feet above the water's surface, making for superb views as you walk around the perimeter of this 38-acre body of water. Be sure to look for the polished rocks and scratches that were made by the glaciers.

Two magnificent hotels once stood within view of each other at the top of the bluffs—the Cliff House to the east, and Wildmere to the northwest. Both hotels were built by Alfred H. Smiley, who along with his twin brother, Albert, was also responsible for creating the Mohonk Mountain House and the Mohonk Mountain Preserve. Gradually, Smiley's Minnewaska property increased to 10,000 acres of land.

In 1955 descendants of the Smiley family sold the land to Kenneth Phillips, the general manager of the Minnewaska Resort. Phillips tried to increase business revenue by adding a golf course just west of the lake in 1957 and by creating a downhill ski area called Ski-Minne in 1963. Despite Phillip's efforts, however, the business failed to do well, and in 1971 a significant portion of the land was sold to the Palisade Interstate Park Commission for the eventual creation of Minnewaska State Park. This sale did not include the area directly around Lake Minnewaska, however, which Phillips still hoped could be turned into a profit if the right buyer came along.

In 1978 the Cliff House burned down, followed eight years later by the Wildmere, which had been closed since 1980. As with the Catskill Mountain House at Pine Orchard in the northern Catskills, virtually no traces remain of these structures.

In 1979 the Marriott Corporation attempted to purchase 500 acres of land around Lake Minnewaska for development. Their vision was to erect a modern, 450-room hotel where the Wildmere once stood, build a conference center, expand the pre-existing golf course into an 18-hole championship golf course, and construct 300 condominiums on the site of the Cliff House. There were public and environmental concerns about how the complex of proposed buildings would obtain sufficient water without depleting Lake Minnewaska or tapping out the limited flow of the Peters Kill. Undoubtedly, though, it was the Marriott Corporation's proposal to build condos near the lake that finally caused a huge public outcry and awakened understanding that this area of the Shawangunks was in danger of being substantially altered and made inaccessible to all but a few individuals.

Realizing that public opinion was turning against them and not wanting to invest additional time and money in further legal battles, the Marriott Corporation decided that too many obstacles had been thrown in their way and they backed off. After years of wrangling, the property was purchased by the Palisades Interstate Park Commission in 1987 and the park was made whole, preserving the entire area in the public domain.

Directions to Minnewaska State Park: From New Paltz drive west on Rt. 299 for approximately 6 miles. When you get to Rt. 44/55, turn right and drive uphill, going first north and then west. After 4.6 miles you will reach Minnewaska State Park, on your left.

Along the way, at 0.5 mile from Rt. 299, you will pass by the Mohonk Visitor Center on your right, which is well worth the stop.

The Cliff House and the Wildmere hotels
once dominated Lake Minnewaska.

Awosting Falls

Accessibility: Less than 0.3-mile walk from parking lot to top of falls; 0.1-mile descent, continuing on carriage road, to bottom of falls

Degree of Difficulty: Easy

Description: Awosting Falls is formed on the Peters Kill, a medium-sized stream that rises from Lake Awosting and Mud Pond, and flows into Rondout Creek at Alligerville.

At the top of the fall, the Peters Kill plunges over a cliff-like edge and plummets for 80 feet into a pool of water.[1-2] Signs posted near the base of the fall indicate that swimming is prohibited.

Several small cascades can be encountered along the way before you reach the top of the waterfall.

Care must be taken if you venture out to the top of the fall, which is a temptation because the carriage road passes directly by the waterfall's brink. Rock climbers consider a free-fall of 35 feet to be the upper limit of survivability. There is an 80-foot drop at Awosting Falls, so stay back from the edge! Also bear in mind that the waterfall can be especially dangerous in the winter, and that the carriage road leading down to the bottom of the gorge, which sometimes freezes over with thick ice, becomes virtually impassable without crampons unless there is sufficient snow cover.

History: Several gazebos were once strategically placed near the top of the fall, much like the gazebos that adorn the many scenic views and overlooks around Lake Mohonk.

When the Cliff House, and eight years later, the Wildmere were constructed on top of the bluffs overlooking Lake Minnewaska, it was only natural that planners turned their eyes to the nearby Peters Kill as a potential source of hydro-electric power. Awosting Falls might have been selected for power generation were it not for the fact that Sheldon Falls, over 0.5 mile further downstream on the Peters

Kill, provided an even greater vertical drop and was far enough from Lake Minnewaska so as to not be regularly visited by the hotels' strolling guests. Awosting Falls, therefore, was left in its natural state.

Directions: Entering Minnewaska State Park, turn right immediately after passing the tollbooth (and paying a day-use charge during the regular season) and follow a dirt road west for 0.2 mile until you reach the lower parking lot.

Return on foot to the tollbooth, and then follow the main road south for 100 feet, heading toward Lake Minnewaska. As soon as you cross over the Peters Kill, turn left and follow a carriage road east as it parallels the Peters Kill. Within less than 0.05 mile you will come to the top of Awosting Falls.

To get to the bottom, continue following the carriage road as it winds downhill to the base of the waterfall.

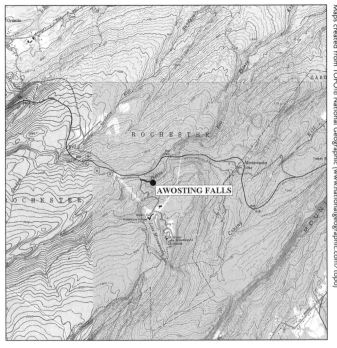

Awosting Falls is 80 feet high.

"Awosting Falls." Minnewaska, N. Y.

Greetings from Minnewaska Agent

No. 1953   Moore & Gibson Co., New York.   (Germany)

Sheldon Falls

Accessibility: 0.8-mile walk from the parking lot to top of the fall; another 0.3-mile walk to bottom of the fall, involving a moderate descent

Degree of Difficulty: Easy to top of fall; Moderate to bottom

Description: Sheldon Falls is formed on the Peters Kill, a medium-sized stream that rises from Lake Awosting and Mud Lake, and flows into Rondout Creek at Alligerville.

Located at the top of the falls is a cement dam that extends across the full width of the Peters Kill. An opening near the center of the dam's spillway now allows water to pass through unobstructed. During conditions of extremely heavy flow, part of the stream is diverted through an opening on the north side of the impoundment, where it follows a streambed until it drops over a cliff edge, plunging back into the Peters Kill far below and producing a secondary waterfall in the process.

Directly above the dam are several small falls and cascades followed by a 15-foot-high cascade—all before the stream reaches the main drop at Sheldon Falls. If you take into account these smaller cascades and drops, Sheldon Falls is well over 100 feet in height.[1-2]

The bedrock at the top of the falls is tilted slightly, causing the water generally to flow along the edge of the north bank.

It is possible to walk behind the cascading waters at the base of the falls, although the amphitheater here is considerably smaller than the one found at Kaaterskill Falls in the Catskills.

Directly across the Peters Kill and not far from the stone foundation at the base of the fall, can be seen a huge cliff face that is generally dry or carrying just a trickle of water. During times of heavy water flow, however, the cliff face produces a secondary waterfall when the main stream overflows and water is tapped off near the dam forming a secondary stream.

Over 0.1 mile downstream from Sheldon Falls can be found a 6-foot waterfall, and 0.1 mile further downstream, a double cascade consisting of a 6-foot drop followed by a 15-foot cascade into a charming glen.

History: At the base of Sheldon Falls stands the stone foundation of an old powerhouse, constructed in 1924, which provided electricity to the two hotels at Lake Minnewaska. During periods of summer drought, when the Peters Kill turned sluggish, electricity was produced through diesel-powered generators. The powerhouse continued operating until the late 1960s. The waterfall was named after Edward Sheldon, the designer of the stone powerhouse. The fall has also been known as Peters Kill Falls.

Near the dam and close to roadside is a stone foundation formed out of huge blocks, the remains of another old structure that was associated with the mountain hotels at Lake Minnewaska.

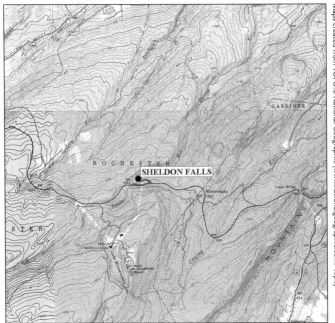

Maps created from TOPO!© National Geographic (www.nationalgeographic.com/topo)

Sheldon Falls.

Directions: At the entrance booth to Minnesawka State Park, immediately turn right and park in the lower parking area at the end of the road. Walk back 0.2 mile and turn right onto the main road, which continues from the entrance booth. Walk south for 100 feet, crossing over the Peters Kill, and then turn left, following the carriage road east as it parallels the south bank of the Peters Kill. You will pass by the top of Awosting Falls in less than 0.05 mile. About 0.5 mile past Awosting Falls, you will come to where the Peters Kill crosses under Rt. 44/55.

To get to the top of Sheldon Falls and its upper cascades, cross over Rt. 44/55 (being sure to keep a sharp eye out for fast-moving vehicles) and walk down a pathway just east of the bridge that leads to a huge expanse of bedrock that constitutes the upper cascades of Sheldon Falls.

To get to the base of Sheldon Falls, walk down Rt. 44/55 going east. Stay off to the side of the road and be ever mindful of traffic. In fact, walk on the other side of the guardrail where possible. In 0.2 mile, just before the guardrail ends, you will come to a faintly outlined, abandoned road on your left that leads down (northwest) to the base of Sheldon Falls within 0.1 mile. Walk carefully, for the road is eroded in places and strewn with blowdown.

To get to the falls below Sheldon Falls, follow an unmarked path downstream that parallels the Peters Kill. At 0.1 mile you will come to the first fall; at 0.2 mile, the second.

Falls on Sanders Kill

Accessibility: 0.6-mile hike round-trip, or 1.6-mile hike round-trip depending on route chosen

Degree of Difficulty: Moderate

Description: These pretty falls are formed on the Sanders Kill, a medium-sized stream that rises north of Lake Awosting and flows into Rondout Creek at Accord. The upper fall is 8 feet high; the lower, 4 feet. Both are formed on a massive block of underlying bedrock.[1]

A small cement barrier less than a foot high can be seen at the top of the upper fall, which suggests that the waterfall was used in past times for purposes other than recreation.

Directions: Although the waterfall is visible from roadside along Rt. 44/55 at 0.9 mile west of the entrance to Minnewaska State Park, guardrails and no-parking signs prevent parking along the side of the road for a lingering view or closer approach. There are two ways to access the falls. One is to continue north on Rt. 44/55 for 1.1 miles from the entrance to Minnewaska State Park (0.2 mile past the fall), and then turn right onto Jenny Lane. Drive east on Jenny Lane (a dirt-packed, unimproved road) for over 0.1 mile, turn right, and continue south for less than 0.1 mile until you come to a small parking area on your right.

From the north end of the parking area, follow a turquoise-blazed trail west, which will take you up to Rt. 44/55 in slightly over 0.2 mile. The walk is very pretty, with mountain laurel on both sides of the trail and an old stone wall. Once you reach Rt. 44/55, the waterfall is 0.1 mile down the road, going south. Stay far to the side of the road as you walk this short distance. Just before you get to the Sanders Kill, a faint path goes off into the woods for 30 feet, with branches leading up to both the base and the top of the waterfall.

The other option is to drive into Minnewaska State Park, turn right after the tollbooth, and park in the westernmost end of the parking area. From the parking lot, begin walking northwest along Rt. 44/55 for 0.8 mile to the waterfall, staying far off to the side of the road.

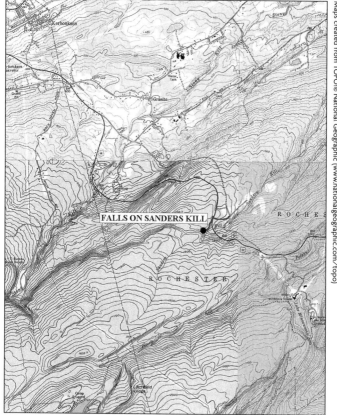

FALLS ON SANDERS KILL

Maps created from TOPO!® National Geographic (www.nationalgeographic.com/topo)

Stony Kill Falls

Accessibility: 0.5-mile walk one-way, mostly on even terrain until the last 0.1 mile, culminating in a tough scramble to get over and around some enormous boulders down from the base of the fall

Degree of Difficulty: Moderate to Difficult

Description: Stony Kill Falls is formed on the Stony Kill, a small stream that rises from several branches along the hills north of Lake Awosting and east of Napanoch Point, and then flows into Rondout Creek at Accord.

Stony Kill Falls is nearly 90 feet in height. If you count the upper cascades, which are not visible from the base of the fall, then the total height is closer to 135 feet. Stony Kill Falls is the second highest waterfall on the Shawangunk Ridge and the highest in Minnewaska State Park. Like Awosting Falls, the main fall consists of a straight plunge off a high cliff edge. Unlike Awosting Falls, however, Stony Kill Falls drops onto a rock-strewn streambed, as opposed to a plunge pool.[1-3]

A small amphitheater has been created under the fall, and it is easy to walk behind the fall without getting wet to enjoy the cataract from other angles. This, of course, is not advisable during periods of torrential rain or in early spring when the waterfall is pounding away at the rock base like a jackhammer.

Huge boulders litter the streambed downstream from the fall, making the hike up to Stony Kill Falls a challenging scamper over and around large boulders. What's nice about this approach to the waterfall, however, as opposed to the much more convoluted one from Lake Awosting, is that you arrive at the bottom of the waterfall, instead of reaching the top where a hazardous descent then has to be made.

Directions: Proceeding along Rt. 44/55 from the southeast, drive 4.3 miles northwest past the entrance to Minnewaska State Park and turn left onto Minnewaska Trail Road. Almost immediately turn left again onto Rock Haven Road.

From the north, leaving Rt. 209, drive southeast on Rt. 44/55 for 1.0 mile and turn right onto Minnewaska Trail Road. Then go 0.5 mile and turn right again onto Rock Haven Road.

Using either approach, drive southwest on Rock Haven Road for 1.9 miles. Turn left onto Shaft 2A Road and continue southwest for 0.3 mile. Bear to the left (basically going straight ahead) where the road divides, and follow it for 0.1 mile, at which point you can park off to the side of the road, making sure that you don't block the gate.

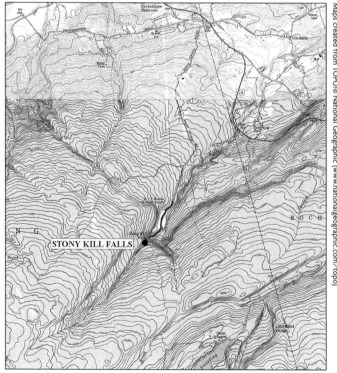

Walk around the gate and continue down the road on foot. This will lead you across a large field and then down into an enormous gravel pit. After walking 0.4 mile, you will reach the opposite end of this large open area where you can follow a trail paralleling Stony Kill for slightly over 0.1 mile to the base of the fall. Be prepared to do some scrambling over large boulders.

If you want a longer hike and are interested in approaching the top of Stony Kill Falls from the main section of Minnewaska State Park, drive into the Lake Minnewaska entrance and park in the lower parking area west of the tollbooth.

Follow the Peters Kill Carriage Road southwest to Lake Awosting—a hike of slightly less than 3 miles. When you reach Lake Awosting, veer right and proceed around the lake for nearly 0.3 mile. Then turn right onto what used to be the Stony Kill Carriageway, but which is now considered an unmaintained trail. Stay on this trail for approximately 0.9 mile and you will come to Fly Brook. Flat Rock, a well-known landmark, will be on your left. Cross over the stream and then bear right at the next fork. (The trail to the left, incidentally, leads to Napanoch Point.) In slightly over a mile you will reach the Stony Kill. Follow the stream down to the top of the fall.

Rainbow Falls

Accessibility: 5.8-mile hike round-trip, mostly following an old carriage road and ending with a short trail down to the fall

Degree of Difficulty: Difficult

Description: Rainbow Falls is formed on a tributary to the Peters Kill, a medium-sized stream that rises from Lake Awosting and Mud Lake, and flows into Rondout Creek at Alligerville. The 75-foot-high waterfall is located in a section of high vertical walls called Huntington Ravine. The name Rainbow Falls arose from the prism-like affect the fall has under the right lighting conditions, breaking the sunlight up into a multitude of colors.[1-4]

Steve Weinman, in *A Rock with a View*, writes that "the forest that you walk through contains some of the oldest trees in the Gunks"[5]—a fact that should add to the overall enjoyment as you wend your way down from the carriage road to the waterfall.

History: As you walk along the numerous, shale carriage roads constructed by the Smileys in the late 1800s and early 1900s, it is worth appreciating just how incredibly durable they have proven to be. The roads were constructed without the use of heavy machinery and would be prohibitively costly were they to be built today. The roads were originally intended for use by horse-drawn carriages taking guests around the grounds of the Mohonk and Minnewaska preserves. Although cars and trucks may have driven on these roads in earlier days, the carriageways are now restricted to pedestrians, and in some places, bicyclists.

Directions: Entering Minnewaska State Park, drive past the toll-booth and continue straight on the main road up to the upper parking area, which is next to Lake Minnewaska.

From the lake, hike west on the Upper Awosting Carriage Road, which is marked with green diamonds. After 2.1 miles you will cross under the Central Hudson power lines. After another 0.5 mile the carriage road descends and crosses over the turquoise-blazed Long Path. At this point veer off to your right, follow the blue-blazed trail downhill for 0.3 mile, and you will reach the fall after fording a small creek across from the waterfall.

If you were to continue on the Upper Awosting Carriage Road, you would eventually reach Lake Awosting, some 0.7 mile west past the detour to Rainbow Falls. Like Lake Minnewaska, Lake Awosting also has had its natural beauty exploited. In 1899, Camp Awosting was erected on the lake and survived as a camp for boys until 1947, when it went bankrupt. Except for some fading ruins, little remains from these past days.

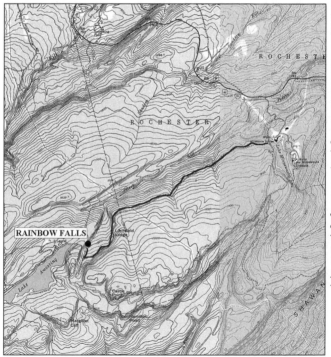

Rainbow Falls, named for its prism-like effect.

Split Rock Falls

Accessibility: Short, level walk

Degree of Difficulty: Easy

Description: Split Rock Falls is a small, flume-created waterfall formed on the Coxing Kill, a medium-sized stream that rises from Lake Minnewaska and flows into Rondout Creek at Lawrenceville. The waterfall has also been called Coxing Kill Falls. The Coxing Kill, named after a local Dutchman, was originally spelled Coxen, with the Dutch word kill added on to indicate a stream.

The waterfall is 8 feet high and situated at the mouth of a narrow chasm some 8 feet wide that extends 40 feet or more through solid, flat bedrock.[1-3]

There is also a small fall further upstream on the Coxing Kill—where the Millbrook Mountain Trail crosses the Coxing Kill—roughly halfway between Lake Minnewaska and Millbrook Mountain.

History: In 1764, Henry Harp was granted a 250-acre plot, which included the area now known as Split Rock Falls. Johannis & Jacob Enderly purchased the lands by the fall in 1801. Records indicate that by 1860 a sawmill was in operation, using the falling waters of the Coxing Kill to power a vertical (up and down) saw. Over time, a tiny community sprang up around the mill and fall and grew to include a blacksmith shop, barrel hoop-making shop, springhouse, barn, and three to four homes.

The land was purchased from the Enderlys by the Mohonk Mountain House Preserve in 1921.

Today the foundations of the Hiram & Loretia Enderly home and the foundation of a large barn can be observed on the walk to the fall. The blade from the sawmill is presently on exhibit at the nearby Trapps Gateway Visitor Center.

Directions: From New Paltz drive west on Rt. 299 for 6 miles, and then turn right onto Rt. 44/55. Follow Rt. 44/55 northwest, proceeding uphill, for 2.1 miles. Turn right onto Clove Road. Drive north for 0.3 mile, veering right at the point where the road divides. After another 0.8 mile turn left into a parking area designated for the preserve.

Walk across the road and follow a wide pathway for several hundred feet that leads past several historic ruins to Split Rock Falls. The fall and flume are directly downstream from the footbridge crossing over the Coxing Kill.

To access the fall further upstream on the Coxing Kill, drive to Minnewaska State Park and park in the upper parking area for Lake Minnewaska. Then take the red-blazed, Lake Shore carriage road south to the south end of the lake. From there proceed south on the red-blazed Millbrook Mountain Trail for roughly 0.7 mile, going steadily downhill for over 300 feet to the Coxing Kill where the small fall can be seen near the point that the trail crosses the stream.

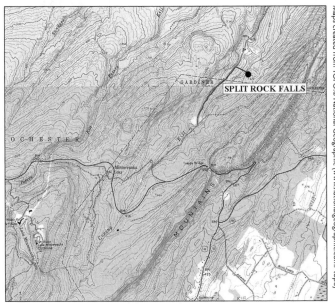

Historic Waterfalls of the Shawangunks

Not all of the falls in the Shawangunks are readily accessible to the public. Some are trail-less and so remote that they cannot be described in a guidebook wherein safety is of paramount concern. Other falls are contained in areas where private ownership prohibits entry. Still, a book on waterfalls would be remiss for not at least mentioning several of these lesser known, "hidden" waterfalls.

Fall in Louis Ravine

This notable waterfall is located in Louis Ravine and is formed on the Beaverkill, a small stream that rises in the hills west of High Point and flows into Rondout Creek near Wawarsing. Marc B. Fried describes it as "a high but nameless fall of water over black shale."[1]

Louis Ravine in 1779 allegedly provided refuge for townsfolk who became alarmed that there might be an Indian attack and, literally, headed for the hills. The ravine has also been known as Witch's Hole.

The upper branches of the Beaverkill are in the general area where huckleberry pickers once established Three Mile Camp along a carriageway on the way up to Napanoch Point.

Palmaghatt Falls

There are several waterfalls of respectable size formed on the Palmaghatt Kill, a small stream that rises in a deep ravine south of Lake Minnewaska and flows into Lake Tillson at Rutsonville. According to sources, there are an upper and lower fall, and several smaller cascades as well. A map included in the New York-New Jersey Trail Conference's *New York Walk Book* (Fifth Edition), indicates that the falls are southwest of Gertrude's Nose.

Palmaghatt Falls is located on property of the Awosting Preserve, a private, nonprofit association that owns 3,000 acres of the Shawangunks. The Awosting Preserve is devoted to forest management and conservation, but their lands are not open to the public and are posted and patrolled. The preserve cannot be entered unless permission is first obtained.

Along
Route 209

Route 209, extending in a southwest/northeast
direction, has been called The Old Mine Road
because of tales told of mines and riches along its
length. The road has also been known as
The Kings Highway, The Queens Highway,
Trade Path, and the Path of the Great Valley.

High Falls

Location: High Falls (Ulster County)

Accessibility: Short walk along descending road that parallels Rondout Creek

Degree of Difficulty: Easy

Description: High Falls is formed on Rondout Creek, a large stream that rises on the eastern shoulder of Rocky Mountain southwest of West Shokan and flows into the Hudson River at Kingston. The fall is approximately 25 feet high, but very broad, capped by a small, fairly unobtrusive dam.[1-2]

The rock composing High Falls consists of Rosendale cement, a carbonate that was formed 410 million years ago and then tilted to its present inclination some 45 million years later. High Falls formed roughly 12,000 years ago when the last glacial retreat diverted the flow of the river from northeast to east, directly over the Rosendale cement bedrock.

A second, smaller waterfall, approximately 10 feet high, drops over a series of ledges a short distance downstream from the main fall.

In the autumn, absolutely gorgeous pictures of High Falls can be taken by standing below the fall, as multicolored trees form a backdrop for its entire length.

History: High Falls is presently used for power generation by the Central Hudson Gas & Electric Corporation. Fortunately, the utility company is civic-minded and has allowed access to the fall through a non-restricted portion of the grounds.

Originally the waterfall was known simply as the Great Falls. Its history goes back as far as 1670. In 1783, Jacob Hasbrouck (or his son, Joseph) built a mill on the north bank. In 1796 two more mills were constructed further down by the lower falls. Later, a couple of fulling mills—for washing and felting homemade woolen cloth— were established on the north and south banks. Historic markers along the walkway by the river point out that there were also cotton and woolen factories, flour, corn, and plaster mills, dyeing works, a leather tannery, and plaster mills at the falls.

Construction of the Delaware & Hudson Canal in 1825 had enormous consequences for the area. Gradually all of the gristmills converted to cement plants because cement was in high demand and was more profitable than grain. Remnants of the old D&H aqueduct can be seen above the fall, and the hulking, stone foundation of an old cement plant is next to the base of the waterfall.

In 1909 a gristmill operated by Abraham Robinson was converted into an electric power generating station. Like Honk Falls to the southwest near Wawarsing, High Falls became a principal supplier of electricity to Kingston, and maintained operations until 1922.

Educational signs posted along the paved walk to the fall and aqueduct provide reams of material on High Falls, the power plant, the aqueduct, and the Delaware & Hudson Canal.

One of the historic signs provides detailed information about the aqueduct that John A. Roebling built downstream from the lower fall in 1849. The structure lasted until 1918, when the less durable upper section, made of timber, was destroyed. The stone arch survived until 1956 when it, too, succumbed and was demolished.

High Falls played a role in the movie *Splendor in the Grass* when Natalie Wood's teenage character almost drowns below the waterfall, an ironic foreshadowing of the actress's tragic fate later in life.[3]

Directions: From Ellenville take Rt. 209 northeast. From the junction with Rt. 44/55 (on your right), continue on Rt. 209 for roughly 10.5 miles further and turn right (east) onto Rt. 213 shortly after passing through Kripplebush.

From Kingston take Rt. 209 southwest for 10 miles, then turn left (east) onto Rt. 213.

Drive east on Rt. 213 for 1.4 miles. As soon as you cross over the bridge spanning Rondout Creek, turn left into the parking lot at the Central Hudson Gas & Electric Corp. A turnstile in the fence allows pedestrians to pass through from the parking lot to a paved road that leads down to the area of the fall.

To access the streambed for an unobstructed view of High Falls, veer left from the paved road at the bottom of the hill and walk toward the river along the fenced perimeter of the cement plant ruins. From there, a short path leads down to the stream. One trail goes straight to the water's edge, where you can see the fall head-on; the other trail goes to the left and leads you along the old, stone cement plant for a closer, lateral look at the fall.

To access the lower fall, return to the paved road and walk down it for another couple of hundred feet. A path leads off to the left to the lower fall.

High Falls, broader than they are high.

Fall on Lower Coxing Kill

Location: Bruceville (Ulster County)

Accessibility: Near roadside

Degree of Difficulty: Easy

Description: This small cascade is formed on the Coxing Kill, a medium-sized stream that rises from Lake Minnewaska and flows into Rondout Creek west of Rosendale.

The waterfall is 6 feet high, block-shaped, and very broad. Interestingly, near the top of the fall at its center is a small tree, which goes to show how tenacious life can be, taking hold even in the most potentially inhospitable places.

History: According to a historic marker near the waterfall, the site presently serving as Captain Schoonmaker's B&B was occupied in 1760 by a home built by Captain Frederick Schoonmaker, who became a Revolutionary War officer. During the war, the home was fortified for defensive purposes. A brochure distributed by the B&B states that "Guests stay in the 1810 Carriage House ... overlooking the trout stream, waterfall, and woodlands."

Directions: From the junction of Rt. 213 East and Rt. 209, drive east on Rt. 213 for 2.7 miles, passing through the small village of High Falls in the process. As soon as you pass by Mossy Brook Road on your right, you will see Captain Schoonmaker's Bed & Breakfast, also on the right-hand side of the road. The fall is just downstream from the Mossy Brook Road bridge. Keep in mind that the fall is on private land.

Fall on Tributary to Coxing Kill

Location: Bruceville (Ulster County)

Accessibility: Roadside

Description: This small waterfall is formed on a tiny tributary to the Coxing Kill just 0.05 mile upstream from the tributary's confluence with the Coxing Kill. The cascade is 10 feet high and slanted, formed on an inclined, hulking bed of rock. A sizeable, rectangular foundation located on the north bank speaks of past industrial times.

History: Bruceville was once a flourishing hamlet, primarily because of the cement works of James Vandemark. Like many of the other tiny hamlets that sprang up and then disappeared along Rondout Creek, Bruceville is contained in a stupendous valley corridor three-fifths of a mile wide that extends all the way from Kingston, past where Rondout Creek veers to the northwest at Napanoch, and down to Port Jervis. It is this valley system that geographically separates the Catskills from the Shawangunks.

Rondout Creek provided a natural waterway for Native Americans, and then later for frontiersmen and trappers. Much later the Delaware and Hudson Canal (the D&H) made use of the valley, bringing anthracite coal from mines in Pennsylvania to Kingston, a distance of 107 miles.

Directions: From the junction of Rtes. 213 East & 209, turn east onto Rt. 213 and drive through the village of High Falls. At 2.7 miles turn right onto Mossy Brook Road and drive south for 0.05 mile. At the junction with Mountain Road, you will see the fall immediately to your left. Take note that the land is posted.

Dashville Falls

Location: Dashville (Ulster County)

Accessibility: Roadside

Description: This dammed waterfall is formed on the Wallkill River, a medium-sized stream that rises in New Jersey near Pochuck Mountain and flows into Rondout Creek northeast of Tillson.

The falls are approximately 30 feet in height, consisting of a number of ledges with a 12-foot-high barrage on top. The Dashville Hydroelectric power plant sits along the east bank of the river at the top of the falls. Because of the amount of water diverted for power generation, the falls are generally lacking animation until water is sufficiently backed up to start going over the top of the spillway.[1]

History: From 1830 to 1835, a flour mill flourished in the hamlet.[2]

Directions: From the intersection of Rtes. 32 & 213, roughly 6 miles northeast of New Paltz, drive northeast on Rt. 213, which is Dashville Road, for 1.0 mile. As soon as you pass Cow Hough Road on your right, turn into a parking area on your left where a sign says "Carry In–Carry Out. Rest Area."

The falls can be seen from this roadside pull-off, but it is best to take along a pair of binoculars since you will find yourself at a significant distance from the falls and dam. You can improve the view appreciably by scrambling down the side of the hill to the edge of the water below.

Additional Point of Interest: Along the way to Dashville Falls, at 0.3 mile from the junction of Rtes. 213 Northeast & 32, sitting virtually next to the NYS Thruway along Rt. 213, is the Perrines Bridge, constructed circa 1844. Although this covered bridge no longer accommodates automobile traffic, pedestrians are permitted to walk across it.

Dashville Falls is "dashing" only during high waters.

Dashville Falls, Rifton, N. Y.

Napanoch/
Wawarsing
Area

Vernooy Kill Falls

Location: Near Cherrytown (Ulster County)

Accessibility: 3.6-mile hike round-trip

Degree of Difficulty: Moderate

Description: Vernooy Kill Falls is formed on the Vernooy Kill, a medium-sized stream that rises northwest of Riggsville and flows into Rondout Creek near Wawarsing.

Vernooy Kill Falls totals 30 feet in height altogether and consists of multiple small cascades along a .05-mile stretch of the stream. The main section of Vernooy Kill Falls can be viewed easily from a footbridge that spans the narrowest part of the stream where it is most chasm-like. There are many ideal spots in the area for a picnic lunch.[1-4]

Old mill foundations and a huge stone wall 15-20 feet high can be seen along the eastern bank just downstream from the foot-bridge.

History: Vernooy Kill Falls was named after Cornelius Vernooy, a settler from Holland who arrived in the Rondout Valley in 1644 and whose family established the first gristmill below the falls in the early 1700s. The mill endured until 1809. It is said that the equipment used by Vernooy was imported from Holland.

The name Wawarsing is Native American for "where the stream flows," an appropriate designation for an area characterized by rushing streams and waterfalls.

Directions: From Rt. 209 at Pine Bush, approximately 1.5 miles north of the junction of Rtes. 209 and 44/55, turn west onto Rt. 3 and drive northwest for 1.3 miles. Then turn left onto Cherrytown Road. Continue west on Cherrytown Road for 3.6 miles and turn left onto Upper Cherrytown Road, just before Cherrytown Road crosses over Mombaccus Creek. Proceed north for another 3.2 miles. You will see a parking area directly to your right, opposite the trailhead to Vernooy Kill Falls, which begins on the left side of the road.

Follow the blue-blazed DEC trail for 1.8 miles to the waterfall area.

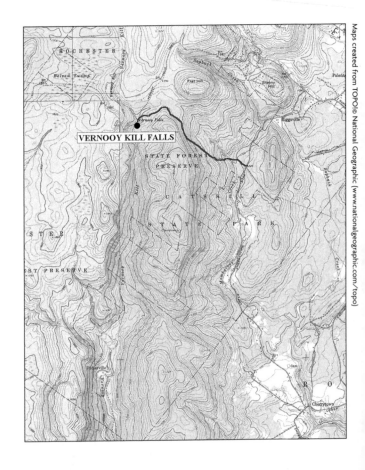

Falls on Mettacahonts Creek

Location: Near Samsonville (Ulster County)

Accessibility: Roadside

Description: This medium-sized, block-shaped waterfall is formed on Mettacahonts Creek, a small stream that rises near Big Rosy Bone Knob and flows into Rochester Creek at Liebhardt. The waterfall is approximately 20 feet high.

A big sign by the road warns that the fall is on private property, and thus should be viewed from roadside only.

History: The village of Samsonville was named after General Henry A. Samson who built a large tannery there.[1]

Directions: From Rt. 209 at Pine Bush, approximately 1.5 miles north of the junction of Rtes. 209 & 44/55, take Rt. 3 for roughly 9 miles to Samsonville. While crossing over a bridge spanning Mettacahonts Creek in the tiny hamlet of Samsonville, you will notice that a waterfall can be seen upstream from the bridge. Unfortunately, there is no public access to the cascade. After the bridge, continue north on Rt. 3 for less than 0.1 mile and turn right onto Browns Rd. Drive southeast for 0.7 mile. The fall will be to your right, just below the point where Kelder Road comes in from the left.

Observe the "no trespassing" sign and stay on the side of the road.

Napanoch Falls

Location: Near Napanoch (Ulster County)

Accessibility: Roadside

Description: Napanoch Falls is formed on Rondout Creek, a medium-sized stream that rises in the hills southwest of West Shokan and flows into the Hudson River at Kingston.

The waterfall is approximately 15 feet in height and fairly broad, extending across the stream for a distance considerably further than at first seems apparent. During summer the waters tend to concentrate near the northern end of the streambed, dropping into a flume roughly 8-9 feet deep.

You will notice a dilapidated, aluminum-framed building along the northern bank at the fall, and an old stone building along the southern bank that once was occupied by D&M Furniture. The area above the falls has been extensively modified by cement channels and a small impounded lake that contains a tiny fall at its inlet.

Directions: From Ellenville drive northeast on Rt. 209 and turn left (west) at Napanoch onto Rt. 55. Proceed uphill for approximately 0.2 mile and park at the intersection of Rt. 55 and Water Street. The falls are directly to your left and visible from roadside, particularly during the early spring or late fall when the foliage is sparse.

Bear in mind that the land is posted. Remain at roadside.

Napanoch Falls.

NAPANOCH STREAM, NAPANOCH, N.Y.

Honk Falls

Location: Napanoch (Ulster County)

Accessibility: Roadside

Description: Honk Falls is formed on Rondout Creek, a medium-sized stream that rises on the eastern shoulder of Rocky Mt. south-west of West Shokan, and flows into the Hudson River at Kingston.

According to Arthur Adams, in *The Catskills*, the falls are 70 feet high.[1] Nathaniel Bartlett Sylvester, in *History of Ulster County, New York,* describes the falls as being 75 feet in height, and states:

> "The craggy rocks on each side of the stream extend to a very great height, and those along the bed of the stream are wrought into every imaginable variety of shapes and forms by the action of the water, assisted by loose stones or gravel, which in working or whirling round by the action of the water have, in some places, worn deep cavities into the solid rock which are truly remarkable."[2]

Honk Falls is located about halfway up an enormous gorge whose bedding is highly tilted, with towering walls on both sides. Just above the falls is a dam at the outlet to Honk Lake. Further upstream, over 4 miles from Honk Lake and at an elevation of 1,440 feet, is Rondout Reservoir.

History: Years ago a hydroelectric plant siphoned off energy from the stream and falls for power generation. Like High Falls to the northeast, Honk Falls was one of the principal suppliers of hydroelectric power to Kingston until 1922. Although the power company is gone, the stone building near the bridge remains and is privately owned.

As to how the waterfall acquired its name, the name Honk

goes back at least several centuries to when a nearby fortification, Fort Honk, was used for defense against Indian attacks.

Directions: From Ellenville proceed northeast on Rt. 209. When you come to Napanoch, turn west (left) onto Rt. 55 and drive uphill for 0.9 mile. The fall will be visible to your right as you cross over a bridge spanning Rondout Creek, though it is quite some distance from the road and at the back of a deep gorge.

Park off to the side of the road and return on foot to the bridge, where a sidewalk on the bridge allows you to view the gorge and falls safely.

Honk Falls, possibly named for colonial Fort Honk.

Ellenville
Area

Ellenville is a fairly large town located in a valley
nestled between the Shawangunk Mountains and
the Allegheny Plateau. The town was named after
Ellen Snyder, sister of Mrs. Nathan Hoornbeck,
one of the community's leading citizens. Ellenville
was originally known as The City, or Fairchild City.

Verkeerder Kill Falls

Location: Sam's Point and Ice Cave Mt. (Ulster County)

Accessibility: 5.6-mile hike round-trip; fee required. The falls are on private property and are not part of the Sam's Point Dwarf Pine Ridge Preserve, but are currently accessible on a marked trail through the preserve.

Degree of Difficulty: Difficult

Description: Verkeerder Kill Falls is an impressive, unspoiled waterfall formed on the Verkeerder Kill, a small stream that rises southeast of High Point and flows into the Shawangunk Kill at Ulsterville. The fall is over 72 feet high.[1-2]

In *Tales from the Shawangunk Mountains*, Marc B. Fried describes an imaginary trip over Verkeerder Kill Falls: "The stream begins to gather itself in a crescendo of gurgling, and a first brilliant flash of white sky announces the great precipice, dead ahead. The unknowing visitor may well be incredulous at first, searching left and right for a route that seems more in touch with reality. But the wind hurling up from unseen depths below rises to a gale, the streambed itself becomes a stark horizon against the open void, and in a great, final, and irretrievable moment the water plunges outward into the deep, open gorge of the lower Verkeerder Kill.[3]

The fall also has been known as Kitykill Falls and Kaidy Kill Falls.[4] The name Verkeerder is Dutch and implies a sense of being twisted, turned, or contorted, which seems appropriate for an area that is gnarly and unlike anything else you are likely to see in the northeast.

Verkeerder Kill Falls are accessed from the Sam's Point Dwarf Pine Ridge Preserve, which is owned by the Open Space Institute of New York and operated by the Nature Conservancy. At one time Sam's Point was a commercial tourist attraction on Ice Cave Mountain, featuring an enormous buttress of rock with fantastic views and the famous ice caves to the east. The current preserve encompasses 4,600 acres of land, including 5 miles of hiking trails and 6 miles of carriage roads, and has been designated one of "Earth's Last Great Places" by The Nature Conservancy.

The dwarf pine barrens consist of acres of small, bonsai-like pitch pines some 6 feet in height. If you are hiking in the fall, you will notice patches of a vivid, crimson color complementing the brilliant white of the Shawangunk conglomerate. This is the autumn finery of the Shawangunks' famous blueberry bushes.

There is a per-person fee in order to access the preserve. Day use only is permitted.

History: Sam's Point was named after Sam Gonzales, who supposedly jumped off the cliffs to avoid being captured by a pursuing party of Indians and landed amongst hemlocks, thereby surviving and making good his escape.

Sam's Point, like other sections of the Gunks, has seen its share of development in the past, but fortunately has been allowed to return to its former, semi-natural state. Back in the 1800s, Thomas Botsford built a hotel on the summit of Sam's Point. Almost immediately after his hotel burned down, another hotel was built, this time just below the summit. The new hotel was 92 feet long and roughly 25 feet wide. Within a few years it, too, was destroyed by fire, and no further hotels were built.

In 1967 the town of Ellenville leased the land at Sam's Point to a commercial organization that ran the attraction for many years as Ice Caves Mountain. This enterprise lasted until 1996.

Directions: From Ellenville (Rt. 209) take Rt. 52 southeast, driving uphill into the upper regions of the Shawangunk Mountains for roughly 5 miles. Turn left onto Sam's Point Road/Cragsmoor Road and proceed upward, following signs that will lead you to the parking area at Sam's Point & Ice Cave Mt., nearly 3 miles from Rt. 52.

From the nature center at the head of the parking lot, walk past an old stone gate, turn right, and follow an eroded asphalt road uphill for 0.6 mile. A left-hand turn will take you to Sam's Point, from where superb views can be obtained of the Wallkill Valley, the Port Jervis trough, the Allegheny Plateau, and the ridge to the southwest. Continue straight past Sam's Point for another 0.4 mile and then turn right onto a road that immediately proceeds downhill, eventually leading to the famous ice caves. Look for a turquoise/blue trail marker on your left indicating the way to Verkeerder Kill Falls. Follow the well-marked trail for 1.8 miles and you will arrive at the waterfall. Along the way you will have wonderful views of Gertrude's Nose and Castle Point (both contained in the Minnewaska Preserve) to the northeast, and also of the Wallkill Valley to the east and southeast, and beyond that, the Hudson Valley.

The path leads through a rare dwarf pine barren, one of only a few remaining in the world. Also take note that this section is part of the famous Long Path.

There is a second approach to Verkeerder Kill Falls, but it is considerably longer and involves hiking in on the Long Path from the southeast end of Lake Awosting to Mud Pond, and from there, continuing on southeast to the fall. This approach, involving a hike of over 10 miles round-trip from the parking area at Lake Minnewaska, really only makes sense if you happen to be at Lake Awosting to begin with.

Additional Point of Interest: While at Sam's Point, don't miss a visit to the spectacular ice caves located just down the road from the trailhead to Veerkerder Kill Falls. The ice caves were formed thousands of years ago when huge blocks of Shawangunk conglomerate broke off when the weaker, underlying shale beds were eroded away. The configuration of toppled blocks forms what is more accurately called a "rock house" (like Rock City Park in Olean, New York), where the blocks are analogous to city buildings, and the passageways between, to city streets. All of this is short-lived, geologically speaking, for the tumbles of blocks are slowly working their way down the slope into the valley below.

If you are interested in delving further into ice caves, Bob McElroy's article on "Exploring Formidable Terrain: The Shingle Gully Ice Caves"[5] provides interesting material on a huge, fissure-created chasm northwest of Sam's Point, called the Ellenville Ice Caves. A permit must be obtained to access the area.

Verkeerder Kill Falls is wild and remote.

Nevele Falls

Location: Ellenville (Ulster County)

Accessibility: Roadside

Description: Nevele Falls is formed on a small stream rising east of Cragsmoor that flows into the Delaware & Hudson Canal at Ellenville.

The waterfall is over 50 feet high and is quite spectacular during snow melt. Ruins of an old factory are evident downstream from the base of the fall. An old footbridge crosses the creek a short distance upstream from the top of the waterfall. Along the north bank downstream from Nevele Falls is an old mine shaft that enters into the side of the ravine, but peters out quickly.

Take note that the property surrounding the fall is posted, but fortunately, the view from the bridge is more than adequate for taking in its splendor.

There is also a waterfall on the grounds of the Nevele Resort Country Club, which guests of the resort are allowed to visit. The Nevele Resort is off Rt. 209 south of Ellenville.

History: According to historical accounts, the waterfall was named by a group of teachers who used to meet at the fall for weekend picnics. Since there were eleven teachers in the group, they decided to name the falls Nevele, which is eleven spelled backwards. The name later spawned Nevele Acres and the Nevele Resort & Country Club. The fall also has been known as Reservoir Falls.

Directions: From Rt. 209 in the center of Ellenville, turn east onto Rt. 52 and proceed as though you were driving up to Sam's Point and Ice Cave Mt., continuing for 1.0 mile from the village. You will cross over a small stream just after where the road turns southeast and begins going uphill. Look to the left and you will see the fall.

Park off to your right on a side street and return to the bridge on foot for a more leisurely look.

406A:-NEVELE FALLS, ELLENVILLE, N. Y.

Nevele is "eleven" spelled backwards.

Tomsco Falls Park

Location: Near Mountain Dale (Sullivan County)

Accessibility: Roadside

Description: Tomsco Falls is formed on Taylor Brook, a tiny tributary to Sandburg Creek. The multi-tiered waterfall, some 80-90 feet high, has been depicted on old postcards with the caption, "The Niagara of Sullivan County."[1-3]

History: The falls also have been known as Little Falls in the past. At one time Rashkin's Little Falls Hotel operated near the falls.

According to Derek Doeffinger & Keith Boas, Tomsco is an acronym for Tuscarora, Oneida, Mohawk, Seneca, Cayuga, and Onondaga—the Six Nations of the Iroquois—and the falls have served as a backdrop for the Miss New York State Pageant, the *Geraldo Rivera Show,* and Trident chewing gum commercials.

Directions: From Ellenville (junction of Rtes. 209 & 52) drive southwest on Rt. 209 for 4.6 miles and turn right onto Old Rt. 209. In less than 0.1 mile, turn right and then, after 0.2 mile, left onto Rt. 55 (which starts off as Rt. 80). From here drive west on Rt. 55 (Mountain Dale Road), which parallels Sandburg Creek. At 5.4 miles from Rt. 209, you will see the falls to your left. Take note that the land is posted, but part of the falls is clearly visible from roadside.

The owner of the falls had at one time turned the property into a nature preserve with guided tours, but was forced to stop the tours when liability issues became a concern.

If you are interested in seeing another nearby waterfall from roadside, continue west on Rt. 55 for 0.9 mile further. At 0.1 mile, before you reach Park Hill Road, pull over to the side of the road. An 8-foot-high cascade contained in a deep ravine can be seen to your right. Remain on the roadside to view this waterfall.

"The Niagara of Sullivan County."

Cascades at Fallsburg

Location: Fallsburg (Sullivan County)

Accessibility: Roadside

Description: The falls at Fallsburg consist of a series of small, but pretty cascades formed on the Neversink River, a medium-sized stream that rises from several branches northeast of the Neversink Reservoir and flows into the Delaware River south of Port Jervis. The falls have also gone by the name of Old Falls.[1-3]

When the water level is low, interesting potholes can be observed in the streambed. Look closely and you will see one particularly large pothole in the upper rocks along the west bank of the stream.

Old foundation walls jut up along the east bank just upstream from the bridge.

At one time the Neversink was a powerful and dynamic river and indeed quite a force to be reckoned with. All this changed, however, when the Neversink Reservoir, some five miles long and over one mile wide, was created in 1955, siphoning off massive amounts of water for downstate use and causing the section of the Neversink River below the reservoir to become an anemic version of its former self.

History: In the early 1800s industries began to be attracted to Fallsburg. A sawmill was built by Herman Ruggles and a gristmill by Henry Reed. In 1809 both businesses were bought out by Thomas S. Lockwood, who is known as "the father of Fallsburg." For a short period of time, the village was called Lockwoods Mills. In 1826, however, the town officially became known as Fallsburg, named for its falls, with the English suffix "burg" for "town" added on.

A large dam above the falls once impounded a millpond. The pond was used by a nearby gristmill and leather tannery. The dam is no longer in existence.

An old, stone, arch bridge, built in 1819, spanned the gorge directly below the falls. The bridge was damaged by heavy waters in 1869, 1883, and 1895, but was successfully brought back to life each time. In 1903 the main stone arch had to be replaced when the middle section of the bridge was washed out. In 1952, however, the historic bridge was replaced by a common, steel and concrete bridge, and an irretrievable piece of history was lost forever.[4]

Directions: From Ellenville (junction of Rtes. 209 & 52) drive northwest on Rt. 52 past Greenfield Park and Dairyland for roughly 12 miles until you reach Woodbourne at the junction of Rtes. 52 and 42. Turn left onto Rt. 42 and drive south for 2.0 miles until you reach the intersection of Rtes. 42 and 52 (this is a different Rt. 52 from the one you just left). Turn left onto Rt. 53 (which is opposite Rt. 52) and immediately cross over the bridge, which spans the Neversink River. Park in the pull-off to your right at the end of the bridge. The main views are from the north side of the bridge, which overlooks the cascades.

Take note of the "No swimming, loitering, or camping" sign by the falls.

On the drive back to Ellenville, as you proceed east along Rt. 52, be sure to look for a series of small cascades that are visible to your left as you cross over a bridge at 7 miles from the junction of Rtes. 42 & 52. The cascades are 6 feet and 4 feet high, respectively, and are formed on the West Branch of Rondout Creek.

About the Author

Russell Dunn, a New York State Licensed Guide, has written more books on waterfalls than any other author in the world, and was profiled by the Associated Press in 2007 in a national feature article. His other works include four guidebooks to the waterfalls of eastern New York State and western Massachusetts: *Adirondack Waterfall Guide: New York's Cool Cascades* (Black Dome Press, 2003); *Hudson Valley Waterfall Guide: From Saratoga and the Capital Region to the Highlands and Palisades* (Black Dome Press, 2005); *Mohawk Region Waterfall Guide: From the Capital District to Cooperstown and Syracuse* (Black Dome Press, 2007); and *Berkshire Region Waterfall Guide: Cool Cascades of the Berkshire & Taconic Mountains* (Black Dome Press, 2008).

He is also the author of *Adventures around the Great Sacandaga Lake* (Nicholas K. Burns Publishing, 2002), and co-author with his wife, Barbara Delaney, of *Trails with Tales: History Hikes through the Capital Region, Saratoga, Berkshires, Catskills & Hudson Valley* (Black Dome Press, 2006). Dunn is currently working on four new guidebooks to the region's trails and waterways.

List of Waterfalls

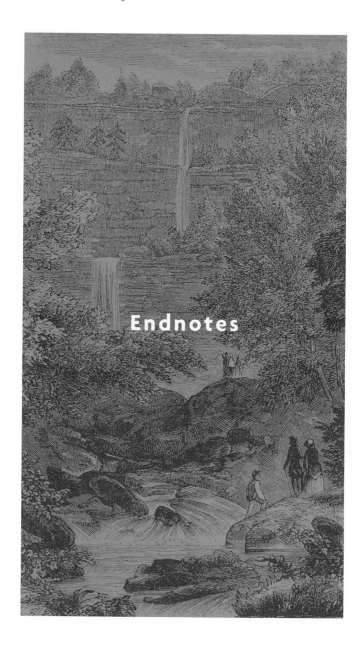

Endnotes

Waterfalls of the Catskills

1. John Lyon Rich, *New York State Museum Bulletin: Glacial Geology of the Catskills* (Albany, New York: The University of the State of New York, 1934), 135.

Falls in Sleepy Hollow Notch

1. Roland Van Zandt, *The Catskill Mountain House* (Hensonville, New York: Black Dome Press Corp, 1993), 79.

2. Washington Irving and Misc. Other Eminent Writers, *The Scenery of the Catskill Mountains* (Facsimile Reprint, Astoria, New York: J.C. & A.L. Fawcett, Inc., no date), 7.

3. Rev. Charles Rockwell, *The Catskill Mountains and the Region Around* (Reprint, Saugerties, New York: Hope Farm Press, 1973), 326.

4. In R. Lioner De Lisser, *Picturesque Catskills: Greene County*, reissued with index and foreword by Alf Evers (Saugerties, New York: Hope Farm Press, 1971), two photos of the ravine and falls, labeled "At the foot of Sleepy Hollow" and "In Sleepy Hollow Ravine," respectively, can be found on page 50, and there is a winter picture of a falls on Stony Brook on page 35.

Kaaterskill Clove

1. Robert Titus, "The Great Cascade," *Kaatskill Life* Vol. 16, No. 3 (Fall 2001), 54.

2. J. Van Vechten Vedder, *History of Greene County, New York, 1651-1800* (Reprint, Saugerties, New York: Hope Farm Press, 1985), 98.

3. Roland Van Zandt, op. cit., 123.

Historic Waterfalls of Palenville

1. Dennis Squires, in *New York Exposed: The Whitewater State* Volume 2 (Margaretville, New York: A White Water Outlaw Publishing, 2003), page 126, shows a picture of a kayaker going over the fall under the Rt. 32 bridge next to the Waterfall Motel.

Waterfalls in Lower Kaaterskill Clove

1. Raymond Beecher and Harvey Durham, *Images of America: Around Greene County and the Catskills* (Dover, New Hampshire:

Arcadia Publishing, 1997), 67.

2. A picture of the tollgate at the entrance to Kaaterskill Clove can be seen in Leah Showers Wiltse's book *Pioneer Days in the Catskill High Peaks: Tannersville and the Region Around* (Hensonville, New York: Black Dome Press Corp., 1999), 41.

Moore's Bridge Falls

1. There is a wonderful old-time illustration of the falls and an early, rustic bridge spanning the creek in an insert between pages 16 & 17 in *The Scenery of the Catskill Mountains,* op. cit.

2. In R. Lionel De Lisser's *Picturesque Catskills: Greene County,* op. cit., a picture of the falls and bridge can be seen on page 40.

3. An illustration of Moore's Bridge and falls entitled "Cascades at the High Rock" can be found on page 250 in *The Catskill Mountains and the Region Around,* by Rev Charles Rockwell, op. cit.

Fawn's Leap

1. According to Edward G. Henry, in *Catskill Trails: A Ranger's Guide to the High Peaks. Book One: The Northern Catskills* (Hensonville, New York: Black Dome Press Corp., 2000), page 65, "Racing down a vertical sandstone wall, the water drops 30 feet. Below its smooth, banked sides, the water fills a crystal-clear, 12-foot-deep pool."

2. In *Catskill Rambles* (Woodstock, New York: The Overlook Press, 1992), page 81, Kenneth Wapner talks about his uncle "walking off the forty foot ledge of Fawns Leap and plummeting into the deep, gravel-bottomed pool."

3. R. Lionel De Lisser, op. cit., 34.

4. Rev Charles Rockwell, op. cit., 302.

Along the South Rim of Kaaterskill Clove

1. Bruce Wadsworth & The Schenectady Chapter of the Adirondack Mountain Club, *Guide to Catskill Trails: Catskill Region* (The Adirondack Mountain Club, Inc., 1988), 50.

2. Lee McAllister, *Hiking the Catskills* (The New York-New Jersey Trail Conference, 1989), 178.

3. Roland Van Zandt, op. cit., 125.

4. Bruce Wadsworth & The Schenectady Chapter of the Adirondack Mountain Club, op. cit., 56.

5. A picture of Santa Cruz Falls can be seen in R. Lionel De Lisser's *Picturesque Catskills: Greene County,* op. cit., 47.

Waterfalls of Upper Kaaterskill Clove

1. Roland Van Zandt, op. cit., 127-28.

Naiad's Bath

1. A picture of the falls can be seen in R. Lionel De Lisser's *Picturesque Catskills: Greene County,* op. cit., 42.

The Five Cascades

1. A superb line drawing of the Five Cascades can be found in *The Scenery of the Catskill Mountains,* op. cit., 45.

2. In *Catskill Trails: A Ranger's Guide to the High Peaks. Book One: The Northern Catskills,* op. cit., page 70, Edward G. Henry states that "the falls, one of well over one hundred feet, lie almost forgotten among the depths of Kaaterskill Clove."

3. Rev. Charles Rockwell, op. cit., 345-46.

Haines Falls

1. A picture of the falls can be seen in Raymond Beecher and Harvey Durham's *Images of America: Around Greene County and the Catskills,* op. cit., 69.

2. Edward G. Henry, op. cit., 70.

3. A picture of Haines Falls as seen from Inspiration Point can be found in Ron Decker's article, "The Elusive Haines Falls," *Kaatskill Life* Vol. 13, No.1 (Spring 1998), 26.

Bastion Falls

1. Edward G. Henry, in *Catskill Trails: A Ranger's Guide to the High Peaks. Book One: The Northern Catskills,* page 66, describes Bastion Falls as "a collection of falls, cascades, steep rock faces, and tumbling roaring water."

2. Derek Doeffinger and Kenneth Boas, in *Waterfalls of the Adirondacks & Catskills* (Ithaca, New York: McBooks Press, 1997),

page 122, state that "the falls cascade in three interesting steps."

3. Bruce Wadsworth & The Schenectady Chapter of the Adirondack Mountain Club, op. cit., 58.

4. In *Catskill Day Hikes for All Seasons* (Lake George, New York: Adirondack Mountain Club, Inc., 2002), page 47, Carol and David White write: "Everything here is big—boulders, huge trees and their root systems, shale cliffs rising across the stream, and, of course, the falls. The water flows over red rock; dripping mosses sparkle in the sun. This is wild, rugged territory."

Kaaterskill Falls

1. The height of Kaaterskill Falls usually is estimated as being 260 feet, with a 180-foot upper fall and an 80-foot lower fall. Robert Gildersleeve, however, in his forthcoming book on the historic hiking trails of Kaaterskill Clove (Black Dome Press, 2005) quotes from a 28 August 1992 letter by James West, then-superintendent of the Bureau of Real Property of New York State Department of Environmental Conservation, in which West cites a 1992 measurement by DEC surveyors that determined the falls' height to be 166.6 feet (upper fall) and 64.1 feet (lower fall), for a total height of 230.7 feet.

2. Clay Perry, in *Underground Empire: Wonders and Tales of New York Caves* (New York: Stephen Daye Press, 1948), page 151, describes Kaaterskill Falls as "leaping off a ledge of the Clove, beneath Sunset Rock, dropping like a rainspout stream, veiling behind its spraying cloud of water some tiny shelf caves, and forming ice caves in winter that reluctantly melt until May."

3. J. Van Vechten Vedder, op. cit., 99-100.

4. *The Scenery of the Catskill Mountains*, op. cit., 36.

5. Edward G. Henry, op. cit., 69.

6. *The Scenery of the Catskill Mountains*, op. cit., 23.

Ashley Falls

1. In *Guide to Catskill Trails: Catskill Region*, op. cit., page 67, Bruce Wadsworth & The Schenectady Chapter of the Adirondack Mountain Club state that "several slabs of rock lean at sharp angles. Above, two upper pitches of the falls can be seen."

2. Roland Van Zandt, op. cit., 115.

3. *Catskill Center News* (May-June 1980), p. 15.

4. Leah Showers Wiltse, op. cit., 100-01.

5. According to Jon Binder at Jon's Waterfalls of the Eastern United States (www.people.cornell.edu/pages/jab244) "Ashley Falls is an interesting waterfall. There are three distinct parts to it. The uppermost is the highest and most vertical drop; then, the water travels over another ledge, before sliding down a slab of rock at a sharp angle."

Platte Clove

1. Frank Oppel, ed., "The Catskills," *New York Tales of the Empire State* (Secaucus, New Jersey: Castle, 1988), 300.

2. Arthur Adams, et al., *Guide to the Catskills* (New York: Walking News, Inc., 1975), 407.

3. Edward G. Henry, op. cit., 33.

4. Edward G. Henry, in *Catskill Trails: A Ranger's Guide to the High Peaks. Book One: The Northern Catskills,* op. cit., 48-49, describes the fascinating geology of Platte Clove.

5. Alf Evers, *The Catskills: From Wilderness to Woodstock* (Woodstock, New York: The Overlook Press, 1982), 446.

6. R. Lionel De Lisser, op. cit., 77.

7. Pictures of Platte Clove waterfalls can be seen in Arthur G. Adams, ed., *The Hudson River: From Tear of the Clouds to Manhattan* (New York: The Monacelli Press, Inc., 1995), 110-11.

8. A picture of Plattekill Falls by Robert Titus can be seen in "The Other Clove," *Kaatskill Life* Vol. 14, No 1 (Spring 1999), 61.

9. Tom Teich's picture of Plattekill Falls can be seen on the back cover of *Kaatskill Life* Vol. 7, No. 1 (Spring 1992).

Hell's Hole

1. A picture of Hell's Hole and Rainbow Falls can be seen in *Picturesque Catskills: Greene County,* op. cit., 67-68.

2. A picture of the "Plaaterkill Falls Mountain House" can be seen in *Picturesque Catskills: Greene County,* op. cit., 158.

3. Alf Evers, op. cit., 233.

Old Mill Falls

1. A picture of the falls, entitled "Falls by Overlook Bridge," can be seen in *Picturesque Catskills: Greene County*, op. cit., 69.

Plattekill Falls

1. Kenneth Wapner, op. cit., 178.

Stony Clove

1. Rev Charles Rockwell, op. cit., page 329, describes the clove as "a deep, narrow pass, through the mountains, shut in on either side by lofty precipices, wild and steep."

Fall in Becker Hollow

1. Edward G. Henry, op. cit., 107.

2. Peter W. Kick, *Catskill Mountain Guide* (Boston: Appalachian Mountain Club, 2002), 36.

Diamond Notch Falls

1. According to Barbara McMartin & Peter Kick in *50 Hikes in the Hudson Valley* (Woodstock, Vermont: Backcountry Publications, 1985), page 168, the falls consist of "several tiers of ten foot or more; succession of large pools."

2. In *Best Hikes with Children in the Catskills & Hudson River Valley* (Seattle: The Mountaineers, 1992), page 169, Cynthia C. & Thomas J. Lewis state that "the West Kill Brook slides down a granite slab to dive 10 feet into a rocky pool." A picture of the waterfall is on page 168.

3. In Lee McAllister's *Hiking the Catskills,* pictures of the fall can be found on pages 154 & 156.

4. In *Guide to Catskill Trails: Catskill Region* by Bruce Wadsworth & The Schenectady Chapter of the Adirondack Mountain Club, op. cit., page 105, Diamond Notch Falls is referred to as a "12-foot plunge of water."

Fall on the Eastkill

1. Peter W. Kick, in *Catskill Mountain Guide,* op. cit., 46, refers to the waterfall as "a little glen and mini-waterfall."

2. Carol & David White, eds., *Guide to Catskill Trails 8* (Lake George, New York: Adirondack Mountain Club, Inc., 2002), 51-53.

3. Doris West Brooks, *The Old Eagle-Nester: The Lost Legends of the Catskills* (Hensonville, New York: Black Dome Press Corp., 1992), 10. A wonderful map of the Eastkill Valley showing the old turnpike from East Jewett to Round Top can be seen on pages 12-13.

4. Leah Showers Wiltse, in *Pioneer Days in the Catskill High Peaks,* op. cit., 101, writes that "Luther Holdridge of Jewett owned a mill in the service woods at the head of the East Kill Valley on the later Colgate property."

Red Falls

1. A picture of Red Falls can be seen in Carol & David White's *Catskill Day Hikes for All Seasons,* op. cit., 58.

2. Dennis Squires, in *New York Exposed: The Whitewater State.* Volume 2, op. cit., page 22 states: "The falls are only 10-12' but they land on solid rock. ... When this river is up (especially when it's high) it takes on a muddy red color."

3. J. Van Vechten Vedder, op. cit., 119.

4. Claire L. Ross & Edward R. Kozacek, *Greene County, New York, 1976 Bicentennial Overview.*

5. Field Horne, T*he Greene County Catskills: A History* (Hensonville, New York: Black Dome Press Corp., 1994), 138-39.

6. Francis P. Kimball, T*he Capital Region of New York State* Vol II (New York: Lewis Historical Publishing Company, Inc., 1942), 370.

Hardenbergh Falls

1. A picture of the falls can be seen on the cover of the August/September 1962 issue of *The Conservationist.*

2. A picture of the fall, along with a caption stating that the view is "near Miss Hardenbergh's Colonial Homestead," can be seen on page 62 in John F. De Vine's *Three Centuries in Delaware County* (New York: Swiss Alps of Delaware County, 1933).

Near Margaretville

1. William M. Gazda, *Place Names in New York* (Schenectady, N.Y.: Gazda Associates, Inc., 1997), 49.

Dry Brook Falls

1. Peggy Turco, in *Walks and Rambles in the Western Hudson Valley* (Woodstock, Vermont: Backcountry Publications, 1996), page 212, describes the first fall as "a waterfall that sluices through a path of green mosses into a bedrock slab pool of turquoise water." On page 213 she locates the second fall when "the road intersects with a well-used private road at a bridge over more enchanting waterfalls." The third fall is mentioned on page 213, but only auditorily: "Pass the sound of more waterfalls in the hemlocks darkening Shandaken Brook."

2. In *Guide to Catskill Trails: Catskill Region,* op. cit., pages 190-91, Bruce Wadsworth & The Schenectady Chapter of the Adirondack Mountain Club state that "A very attractive waterfall is immediately upstream on Dry Brook."

3. Robert Titus, "Dry Brook in Flood," *Kaatskill Life* Vol. 12, No. 1 (Spring 1997), 48. A picture of the middle falls can be seen on page 49.

4. Nathaniel Bartlett Sylvester, *History of Ulster County, New York* (Philadelphia: Everts & Peck, 1880), 329.

Tompkins Falls

1. Robert Titus, "Pepacton: A Winter Voyage," *Kaatskill Life* Vol 18, No. 3 (Fall 2003), 52-58.

2. *History of Delaware County, N.Y.: With Illustrations, Biographical Sketches, and Portraits of Some Pioneers and Prominent Residents* (New York: W. W. Munsell & Co., 1880), 26, 107.

Klein's Falls

1. In *Appalachian Waters 2: The Hudson River and Its Tributaries* (Oakton, Virginia: Appalachian Books, 1974), page 250, Walter F. Burmeister describes the falls as "an 11-foot high ledge formation." On page 253 Burmeister states, "The water tears around a pronounced bend and then cascades furiously down a natural rocky staircase located in a picturesque ravine directly below the bridge."

2. J. Van Vechten Vedder, op. cit., 60.

3. Raymond Beecher and Harvey Durham, op. cit., 67. A photograph of the falls with a long covered bridge at the top of the falls can be seen on page 65.

High Falls

1. Walter F. Burmeister, op. cit., 252.

2. A picture of the falls can be seen in *Images of America: Around Greene County and the Catskills,* op. cit., 66.

3. A picture of the gorge, looking downstream from the top of the bridge as you would view it today, can be seen in an article by Robert Titus entitled "Glacial Lake Albany," *Kaatskill Life* Vol. 17, No. 4 (Winter 2002), 35.

4. Dennis Squires, op. cit., page 125, states "There are a couple of good-sized drops close together, just above the bridge at High Falls. ... The last 150 yards to the brink of this 60 + falls is a fast shallow ledge."

5. High Falls has also been known as Great Falls according to a photograph on page 21 in *Picturesque Catskills: Greene County,* op cit.

6. Arthur G. Adams, *The Hudson River Guidebook* (New York: Fordham University Press, 1996), 245.

Falls at Austin Glen

1. Clay Perry, op. cit., 146-49.

2. In *Appalachian Waters 2: The Hudson River and Its Tributaries,* op. cit., page 197, Walter F. Burmeister writes: "The bridge of New York State Thruway spans the gorge, high above Catskill Creek about one-half mile below the difficult upstream drop. In a number of attractive bends the course continues within the confines of the natural trough, falling temperamentally from ledge to ledge of the vast staircase toward Austin Glen's exit."

3. *Picturesque Catskills: Greene County,* op. cit., page 20, contains a wonderful picture of the old mill in Austin Glen, as well as a photo of the train track wending its way through the glen on page 21.

4. See Alec C. Proskin, *No Two Rivers Alike* (Fleischmanns, New York: Purple Mountain Press, 1995), pages 77-80, for more details on approaching Austin Glen by canoe.

Rip Van Winkle Falls

1. Arthur Adams, et al., *Guide to the Catskills,* op. cit., 226.

2. Raymond Beecher and Harvey Durham, op. cit., 19.

Falls at Woodstock Dam

1. Walter F. Burmeister, op. cit., 193.

2. *Picturesque Catskills: Greene County*, op. cit., shows pictures of the creek, the covered bridge, and the old paper mill and falls on pages 92-93.

Shingle Kill Falls

1. A photo of the falls can be found in *Picturesque Catskills: Greene County*, op. cit., page 80. On page 107, De Lisser states that "The Shingle Kill Falls, located here, on a stream by that name, is one of the principal ones in the county. Below the falls is a romantic ravine." Later De Lisser mentions tramping through the woods to visit Dutchess Falls, Slater's Falls, Forest Ravine Falls, Renny's Glen, and Diana's Well, many or all of which are no longer accessible to the public. How times have changed in over 100 years!

2. Dennis Squires, op. cit., page 211, writes, "There is a 6' ledge drop with a shallow landing right above Route 24/Purling Road Bridge and a 30' falls (Shingle Kill), which is just below the bridge."

Glen Falls

1. *Picturesque Catskills: Greene County*, op. cit., 81. There is also a picture of the fall on page 84. Judging from the picture on page 81, it's quite possible that the fall opposite Glen Falls once may have been known as Slater's Fall.

Artist Falls

1. *Picturesque Catskills: Greene County*, op. cit., contains pictures of Artist Falls on pages 83 & 154.

Fall in East Durham

1. J. Van Vechten Vedder, op. cit., 258.

2. A picture of the fall looking very industrialized can be seen on page 114 in *Picturesque Catskills: Greene County*, op. cit.

Falls at Zoom Flume

1. *I Love New York 2002 New York State Travel Guide*, p. 74.

2. J. Van Vechten Vedder, op. cit., 259.

3. Mary Lynn Blanks, in *Fun with the Family in New York: Hundreds of Ideas for Day Trips with the Kids* 3rd edition (Guilford, Connecticut: The Globe Pequot Press, 2001), page 64, writes: "Slip-slide down a 300-foot water chute, float around the Lazy River, raft the rapids, or wrestle the Mighty Anaconda."

Falls on Sawkill
1. A picture of the falls can be seen in R. Lionel De Lisser's *Picturesque Ulster*, reprinted with index and foreword by Alf Evers (Saugerties, New York: Hope Farm Press, 1968), 228

2. Alf Evers, *The Catskills: From Wilderness to Woodstock*, op. cit., 633.

Falls on Tannery Brook
1. *Picturesque Ulster*, op. cit., contains a picture of the falls on page 233.

2. According to Dennis Squires, op. cit., page 200, "you'll find an 8' falls under Route 212 (and maybe a shopping cart in the pool at the bottom) and a series of class III-IV ledges that march down to the Sawkill."

High Falls
1. A picture of the falls can be seen in *Waterfalls of the Adirondacks & Catskills*, op. cit., 94.

Falls along Peekamoose Road
1. A picture of Buttermilk Falls can be seen in *Best Hikes with Children in the Catskills & Hudson River Valley*, op. cit., page 171, in the chapter titled "Reconnoiter Rock."

2. Another picture of Buttermilk Falls can be seen on page 167 in *Guide to Catskill Trails: Catskill Region* by Bruce Wadsworth & The Schenectady Chapter of the Adirondack Mountain Club, op. cit.

3. A line drawing of the fall can be seen in the New York-New Jersey Trail Conference's *New York Walk Book* Fifth Edition (Garden City, New York: Anchor Press/Doubleday, 1971), 156.

4. *Picturesque Ulster*, op. cit., 149.

5. Marc B. Fried, *The Early History of Kingston and Ulster*

County, NY (Marbletown, New York: Ulster County Historical Society, 1975), 181.

Fall in Ferndale

1. In *Images of America: Sullivan County Borscht Belt,* op. cit., a picture of the falls with a huge dam behind it can be seen on page 13.

Falls on Tributary to Willowemoc Creek

1. Carol & David White, *Catskill Day Hikes for all Seasons,* op. cit., 150: "Beyond, a beautiful large waterfall drops into a shallow pool, enabling the hiker to wade under the sunny spray on a hot day."

Russell Brook Falls

1. A wonderful picture of Russell Brook Falls can be seen in Barbara McMartin & Peter Kick's *Fifty Hikes in the Hudson Valley,* op. cit., 196.

2. Cynthia C. Lewis & Thomas J. Lewis, *Best Hikes with Children in the Catskills & Hudson River Valley,* op. cit., 203, in chapter "Trout and Mud Ponds."

3. Leslie C. Wood, *Holt! T'Other Way!* (Middletown, New York: privately printed, 1950), 186.

Waterfalls of the Shawangunks

Awosting Falls

1. A picture of Awosting Falls, photographed by Herb Chong, can be seen in "The Attraction of Falling Water," *Catskill Mountain Regional Guide* Vol. 18, no. 5 (May 2003), 42.

2. A photograph of the fall can be seen in *Waterfalls of the Adirondacks & Catskills,* op. cit., 77.

Sheldon Falls

1. A picture of the fall can be seen in Edward G. Henry, *Gunks Trails: A Ranger's Guide to the Shawangunk Mountains* (Hensonville, New York: Black Dome Press Corp., 2003), 89.

2. A picture of Sheldon Falls can be seen in Wallace Nutting, *New York Beautiful* (New York: Bonanza Books, 1927), 160.

Falls on Sanders Kill

1. A photograph of the waterfall can be seen in Carr Clifton, *New York: Images of the Landscape* (Englewood, Colorado: Westcliffe Publishers, Inc., 1988), 107.

Stony Kill Falls

1. Jeffrey Perls, *Shawangunks Trail Companion* (Woodstock, Vermont: Backcountry Guides, 2003), 232.

2. A drawing of the falls can be seen in Jack Fagan's *Scenes and Walks in the Northern Shawangunks* (New York: The New York-New Jersey Trail Conference, 1998), 133. According to Fagan, page 132, "Stony Kill Falls, which drains the slab-lands or pine plains, drops 87 feet over conglomerate ledges."

3. According to the New York-New Jersey Trail Conference's *New York Walk Book* Fifth Edition, op. cit., page 135, "From the top the water makes a series of cascades followed by a sheer plunge of 90 feet, a drop of 135 feet in all."

Rainbow Falls

1. Arthur G. Adams, in *The Catskills: An Illustrated Historical Guide with Gazetteer* (New York: Fordham University Press, 1990), page 337, states that "Water flows over several ledges for total drop of 75 feet."

2. In *Walks and Rambles in the Western Hudson Valley*, op. cit., page 159, Peggy Turco states that "Rainbow Falls [is] small but enchanting. Three streams of water dribble over a ledge slapping the stones at your feet."

3. A drawing of Rainbow Falls can be seen on page 146 in *Scenes and Walks in the Northern Shawangunks,* op. cit.

4. A picture of Rainbow Falls, looking very dry, can be seen on page 77 in *Best Hikes with Children in the Catskills & Hudson River Valley,* op. cit. The authors describe Rainbow Falls on page 78 as a place where "a delightful veil of water dives 40 feet. Behind the mist, rainbows shimmer."

5. Steve Weinman, *A Rock with a View: Trails of the Shawangunk Mountains* (New Paltz, New York: Steve Weinman, 1995), 27.

Split Rock Falls

1. In *Shawangunks Trail Companion,* op. cit., Split Rock is described as a "deep, narrow trough in the bedrock ... that empties into a pool perfect for wading."

2. Jack Fagan, in *Scenes and Walks in the Northern Shawangunks,* op. cit., page 87, has sketched a wonderful drawing of the flume.

3. A drawing of the fall on the upper Coxing Kill can be seen on page 120 in *Scenes and Walks in the Northern Shawangunks,* op. cit.

Fall in Louis Ravine

1. *Tales from the Shawangunk Mountains,* op. cit., 31.

High Falls

1. According to Walter F. Burmeister, in *Appalachian Waters 2: The Hudson River and Its Tributaries,* op. cit., page 317, "A 7-foot dam above a 20-foot falls introduces a rocky ravine that reaches downstream to Rosendale. Within this picturesque defile the creek plays hide and seek with tricky ledge formations, boulders, rocks, remnants of dams, steep gravel bars, and constricted chutes."

2. Talking about the lower falls, Dennis Squires, in *New York Exposed: The Whitewater State Volume 2,* op. cit., page 175, states that "You start off at Little Falls (IV), right below High Falls. If you run this drop realize that there are submerged rocks at the base that are hard to see."

3. Patricia Edwards Clyne, *Hudson Valley Tales and Trails* (Woodstock, New York: The Overlook Press, 1990), 123.

Dashville Falls

1. In *Appalachian Waters 2: The Hudson River and Its Tributaries,* op. cit., page 345, Walter F. Burmeister states that the "30-foot ledge formation is tightly edged by the precipitous walls of the gorge."

2. Nathaniel Bartlett Sylvester, op. cit., 115.

Vernooy Kill Falls

1. In *Guide to Catskill Trails: Catskill Region,* op. cit., page 175,

Bruce Wadsworth and the Schenectady Chapter of the Adirondack Mountain Club state, "This interesting waterfall has four cascades dropping a total of about 30 feet."

2. Barbara McMartin & Peter Kick, in *50 Hikes in the Hudson Valley*, op. cit., page 112, state, "Below the mill site, Vernooy Kill continues to tumble over boulders, creating cascades and small falls in the secluded valley."

3. A picture of the falls can be seen in *Best Hikes with Children in the Catskills & Hudson River Valley*, op. cit., 106.

4. A picture of a different section of the falls can be seen in *Walks and Rambles in the Western Hudson Valley*, op. cit., 172. On page 171, Peggy Turco states, "Even in times of severe drought, cold Vernooy Kill runs, dropping about 60 feet over Catskill shale ledges in a series of cascades."

Falls on Mettacahonts Creek

1. Kenneth Wapner in *Catskill Rambles*, op. cit., page 101, describes the falls in Samsonville as being 30 feet tall, and related an encounter with a local who told him about the area's past industrial activities: "He pointed to pilings across the stream, where a grist mill once operated, and explained (amused by my ignorance) that grist is corn, wheat, barley—any pulverized grain. The largest tannery in the country once operated nearby as did a sawmill."

Honk Falls

1. Arthur Adams, in T*he Catskills: An Illustrated Historical Guide with Gazetteer*, op. cit., states that Honk Falls is 70 feet in height.

2. Nathaniel Bartlett Sylvester, op. cit., 269.

Verkeerder Kill Falls

1. A drawing of the falls can be seen on page 170 in *Scenes and Walks in the Northern Shawangunks*, op. cit. On page 153, Fagan states, "The Verkeerder Kill—a shallow, fast moving stream—drops over a spectacular waterfall at the edge of the plateau."

2. From a flat rock at the top of the fall known as Falls View Lookout, "the entire falls can be seen as the water drops seventy-

two feet into a natural amphitheater, with vertical rock walls on three sides and a large pool at the bottom," according to the New York-New Jersey Trail Conference's *New York Walk Book,* Fifth Edition, op. cit., page 137.

3. Marc B. Fried, *Tales from the Shawangunk Mountains,* op cit., 11.

4. Patricia Edwards Clyne, "After the Falls: A Collection of Valley Cascades," *Hudson Valley* (September 1999), 27.

5. Bob McElroy, "Exploring Formidable Terrain: The Shingle Gully Ice Caves," *Kaatskill Life* Vol. 18, No. 2 (Summer 2003), 64-66.

Tomsco Falls Park

1. Mary Lynn Blanks, op. cit., 75.

2. A picture of the falls taken by Scott Zinck can be seen on the cover of *Kaatskill Life* Vol 12, No. 2 (Summer 1997).

3. Derek Doeffinger & Keith Boas, op. cit., 108. There is also a photograph of the falls, with the owners of Tomsco Falls Park standing at the base, on page 109.

Cascades at Fallsburg

1. A picture of a canoe entering the rapids below the falls can be seen in Lawrence I. Grinnell, *Canoeable Waterways of New York State* (New York: Pageant Press, Inc., 1956), between pages 155-56.

2. In Irwin Richman, *Images of America: Sullivan County Borscht Belt* (Charleston, South Carolina: Arcadia Publishing, 2001), a picture of the falls, which locals called Old Falls, can be seen on page 12.

3. James Eldridge Quinlan, in *History of Sullivan County* (Liberty, New York: G.M. Beebe and W.T. Morgans, 1873), page 25, states that "In Fallsburgh, one of the creeks cuts through the red and gray sandstones."

4. Andrew Neiderman, ed., *The Sesquicentennial History of Fallsburg Township: 1826-1976* (South Fallsburg, New York: Town of Fallsburg, 1976), 9. A picture of the original single-arch bridge is presented on page 29.

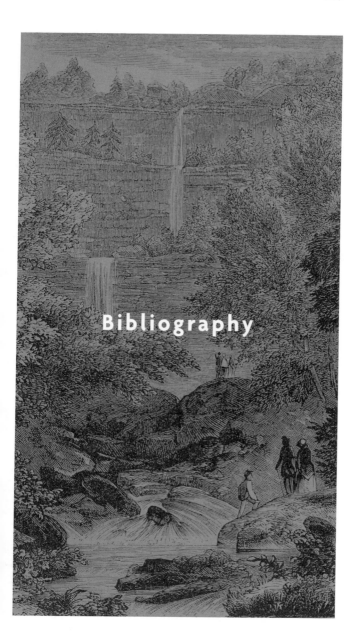

Bibliography

Adams, Arthur G. *The Catskills: A Guide to the Mountains and Nearby Villages.* Fleischmanns, N.Y.: Purple Mountain Press, 1988.

————. *The Catskills: An Illustrated Historical Guide with Gazetteer.* New York: Fordham University Press, 1990.

————. *The Hudson River Guidebook.* New York: Fordham University Press, 1996.

————, ed. *The Hudson River: From Tear of the Clouds to Manhattan.* New York: The Monacelli Press, Inc., 1995.

Adams, Arthur G., Roger Coco, Harriet Greenman & Leon R. Greenman. *Guide to the Catskills.* New York: Walking News, Inc., 1975.

Avery, Marge and Irving & Shirley Fulton, eds. *Livingston Manor Centennial: 1882-1982.*

Beecher, Raymond & Harvey Durham, in conjunction with the Greene County Historical Society. *Images of America: Around Greene County and the Catskills.* Dover, N.H.: Arcadia Publishing, 1997.

Beers, J.B., ed. *History of Greene County, New York.* Reprint, Saugerties, N.Y.: Hope Farm Press, 1969.

Bennet, John & Seth Masia. *Walks in the Catskills.* New York: The East Woods Press, Inc., 1974.

Blanks, Mary Lynn. *Fun with the Family in New York: Hundreds of Ideas for Day Trips with the Kids* (3rd edition). Guilford, Conn.: The Globe Pequot Press, 2001.

Brigham, Albert Perry. *New York State Museum Bulletin: Glacial Geology and Geographic Conditions of the Lower Mohawk Valley.* Albany, N.Y.: University of the State of New York, 1929.

Brooks, Doris West. *The Old Eagle-Nester: The Lost Legends of the Catskills.* Hensonville, N.Y.: Black Dome Press Corp., 1992.

Bulson, Dorwin W. *To-wos-scho-hor: The Land of the Unforgotten Indian.* No publisher, 1961.

Burmeister, Walter F. *Appalachian Waters 2: The Hudson River and Its Tributaries.* Oakton, Va.: Appalachian Books, 1974.

Capossela, Jim. *Good Fishing in the Catskills* (2nd edition). Woodstock, Vt.: Backcountry Publications, 1992.

Catskill Center News. May-June 1980. Hobart, N.Y.: The Catskill

Center for Conservation and Development, Inc.

Chong, Herb. "The Attraction of Falling Water," *Catskill Mountain Region Guide* Vol. 18, No. 5 (May 2003).

Clifton, Carr. *New York: Images of the Landscape.* Englewood, Colo.: Westcliffe Publishers, Inc., 1988.

Clyne, Patricia Edwards. *Hudson Valley Tales and Trails.* Woodstock, N.Y.: The Overlook Press, 1990.

———. "After the Falls: A Collection of Valley Cascades," *Hudson Valley* (September 1999).

Decker, Ron. "The Elusive Haines Falls," *Kaatskill Life* Vol. 13, No. 1 (Spring 1998).

De Lisser, R. Lionel. *Picturesque Catskills: Greene County.* Northampton, Mass.: Picturesque Publishing Company, 1894. Reprinted with an index and foreword by Alf Evers (Saugerties, N.Y.: Hope Farm Press, 1971).

———. *Picturesque Ulster.* Kingston, N.Y.: Styles & Bruyn Publishing Co, 1896-1905. Reprinted with index and foreword by Alf Evers (Saugerties, N.Y.: Hope Farm Press, 1968).

De Vine, John F. *Three Centuries in Delaware County.* New York: Swiss Alps of Delaware County, 1933.

Doeffinger, Derek & Kenneth Boas. *Waterfalls of the Adirondacks & Catskills.* Ithaca, N.Y.: McBooks Press, 1997.

Dunn, Russell. "Hunting for Waterfalls," *Kaatskill Life* Vol. 12, No. 1 (Spring 1997), 32-41.

Ebel, Nancy A. "Hike to Kaaterskill Falls," *Kaatskill Life* Vol. 12, No. 1 (Spring 1997), 26-27.

The Encyclopedia of New York: Vol 2. New York: Somerset Publishers, Inc., 1996.

Evers, Alf. *The Catskills: From Wilderness to Woodstock.* Woodstock, N.Y.: The Overlook Press, 1982.

———. *In Catskill Country.* Woodstock, N.Y.: The Overlook Press, 1995.

———. *Resorts of the Catskills.* New York: The Architectural League of New York, the Gallery Association of New York State, 1980.

Fagan, Jack. *Scenes and Walks in the Northern Shawangunks.* New York: The New York-New Jersey Trail Conference, 1998.

Fallon-Mower, Janine. *Images of America: Woodstock.* Charleston, S.C.: Arcadia Publishing, 2002.

Fried, Marc B. *The Early History of Kingston & Ulster County, NY.* Marbletown, N.Y.: Ulster County Historical Society, 1975.

———.*The Huckleberry Pickers: A Raucous History of the Shawangunk Mountains.* Hensonville, N.Y.: Black Dome Press Corp., 1995.

———. *Shawangunk.* Gardiner, N.Y.: Marc B. Fried, 1998.

———. *Tales from the Shawangunk Mountains.* Glens Falls, N.Y.: Adirondack Mountain Club, Inc., 1981.

Gazda, William M. *Place Names in New York.* Schenectady, N.Y.: Gazda Associates, Inc., 1997.

Gibson, Chuck. *Forty Falls.* Ticonderoga, N.Y.: RA Press, 2003.

Griffin, Irma Mae. *History of the Town of Roxbury.* Roxbury, N.Y.: By author, 1975.

Grinnell, Lawrence I. *Canoeable Waterways of New York State.* New York: Pageant Press, Inc., 1956.

Held, James E. "The Old Mine Road: Fable or Fact?" *Kaatskill Life* Vol. 15, no. 4 (Winter 2000).

Henry, Edward G. *Catskill Trails: A Ranger's Guide to the High Peaks. Book One: The Northern Catskills.* Hensonville, N.Y.: Black Dome Press Corp., 2000.

———. *Catskill Trails: A Ranger's Guide to the High Peaks. Book Two: The Central Catskills.* Hensonville, N.Y.: Black Dome Press Corp., 2000.

———.*Gunks Trails: A Ranger's Guide to the Shawangunk Mountains.* Hensonville, N.Y.: Black Dome Press Corp., 2003.

History of Delaware County, N.Y.: With Illustrations, Biographical Sketches, and Portraits of Some Pioneers and Prominent Residents. New York: W. W. Munsell & Co., 1880.

Horne, Field. *The Greene County Catskills: A History.* Hensonville, N.Y.: Black Dome Press Corp., 1994.

Irving, Washington, & Misc. Other Eminent Writers. *The Scenery of the Catskill Mountains.* Facsimile reprint. Astoria, N.Y.: J.C. & A.L. Fawcett, Inc., n.d.

Jacobson, Alice H. *Beneath Pepacton Reservoir.* Andes, N.Y.: By author, 1988.

Jon's Waterfall Website (Jon Binder): *Jon's Waterfalls of the Eastern U.S.*

Kick, Peter W. *Catskill Mountain Guide.* Boston: Appalachian Mountain Club, 2002.

Kimball, Francis P. *The Capital Region of New York State* Vol. II. New York: Lewis Historical Publishing Company, Inc., 1942.

Lewis, Cynthia C. & Thomas J. Lewis. *Best Hikes with Children in the Catskills & Hudson River Valley.* Seattle: The Mountaineers, 1992.

Mack, Arthur C. *Enjoying the Catskills.* New York: Funk & Wagnalls Company, 1950.

McAllister, Lee. *Hiking the Catskills.* The New York-New Jersey Trail Conference, 1989.

McElroy, Bob. "Exploring Formidable Terrain: The Shingle Gully Ice Caves." *Kaatskill Life* Vol. 18, No. 2 (Summer 2003).

McMartin, Barbara & Peter Kick. *50 Hikes in the Hudson Valley.* Woodstock, Vt.: Backcountry Publications, 1985.

Mitchell, John G. & Charles D. Winters. *The Catskills: Land in the Sky.* New York: The Viking Press, 1977.

Morrison, Wilbur H. *Adventure Guide to the Catskills & Adirondacks.* Edison, N.J.: Hunter Publishing, Inc., 1995.

Mountain Top Historical Society. *Kaaterskill: From the Catskill Mountain House to the Hudson River School.* Hensonville, N.Y.: Black Dome Press Corp., 1993.

Moxham, Lynn. *Geochemical Reconnaissance of Surficial Materials in the Vicinity of Shawangunk Mountains, New York.* Albany, N.Y.: The University of the State of New York/The State Education Department, 1972.

Mulholland, W. D. *Catskill Trails: Recreation Circular 9.* Albany, N.Y.: State of New York Conservation Department, 1964.

Myers, Kenneth. *The Catskills: Painters, Writers, and Tourists in the Mountains 1820-1895.* Yonkers, N.Y.: The Hudson River Museum of Westchester, 1988.

Neiderman, Andrew, ed. *The Sesquicentennial History of Fallsburg Township: 1826-1976.* South Fallsburg, N.Y.: Town of Fallsburg, 1976.

New York-New Jersey Trail Conference. *New York Walk Book* Fifth Edition. Garden City, N.Y.: Anchor Press/Doubleday, 1971.

New York State, I Love New York: 2002 New York State Travel Guide.

Nutting, Wallace. *New York Beautiful.* New York: Bonanza Books, 1927.

Oppel, Frank, ed. "The Catskills." *New York: Tales of the Empire State.* Secaucus, N.J.: Castle, 1988.

Parsons, Greg & Kate B. Watson. *New England Waterfalls: A Guide to More than 200 Cascades and Waterfalls.* Woodstock, Vt.: The Countryman Press, 2003.

Perls, Jeffrey. *Shawangunks Trail Companion.* Woodstock, Vt.: Backcountry Guides, 2003.

Perry, Clay. *Underground Empire: Wonders and Tales of New York Caves.* New York: Stephen Daye Press, 1948.

Proskin, Alec C. *No Two Rivers Alike.* Fleischmanns, N.Y.: Purple Mountain Press, 1995.

Quinlan, James Eldridge. *History of Sullivan County.* Liberty, N.Y.: G.M. Beebe and W. T. Morgans, 1873.

Rich, John Lyon. *New York State Museum Bulletin: Glacial Geology of the Catskills.* Albany, N.Y.: University of the State of New York, 1934.

Richman, Irwin. *Images of America: Sullivan County Borscht Belt.* Charleston, S.C.: Arcadia Publishing, 2001.

Rockwell, Rev. Charles. *The Catskill Mountains and the Region Around.* Saugerties, N.Y.: Hope Farm Press, 1973.

Ross, Claire L. & Edward R. Kozacek. *Greene County, New York. 1976 Bicentennial Overview: Beginnings and Background.* Catskill, N.Y.: Catskill Enterprises, 1976.

Ruth's Waterfall Website: *Ruth's Waterfalls of the Finger Lakes and Rochester, NY.* www.naturalhighs.net

Scheller, William G. & Kay. *New York: Off the Beaten Path* 4th edition. Old Saybrook, Conn.: The Globe Pequot Press, 1977.

Smith, Anita M. *Woodstock: History and Hearsay.* Saugerties, N.Y.: Catskill Mountains Publishing Corporation, 1959.

Squires, Dennis. *New York Exposed: The Whitewater State* Volume 2. Margaretville, N.Y.: A White Water Outlaw Publishing, 2003.

Sylvester, Nathaniel Bartlett. *History of Ulster County, New York: With Illustrations and Biographical Sketches of Its Prominent Men and Pioneers.* Philadelphia: Everts & Peck, 1880.

Titus, Robert. *The Catskills: A Geological Guide.* Fleischmanns, N.Y.: Purple Mountain Press, 1993.

———. *The Catskills in the Ice Age.* Fleischmanns, N.Y.: Purple Mountain Press, 1996.

———. "Dry Brook in Flood." *Kaatskill Life* Vol. 12, No. 1 (Spring 1997).

———. "Glacial Lake Albany." *Kaatskill Life* Vol. 17, No. 4 (Winter 2002).

———. "The Great Cascade." *Kaatskill Life* Vol 16, No. 3 (Fall 2001).

———. "The Other Clove." *Kaatskill Life* Vol. 14, No. 1 (Spring 1999).

———. "Pepacton: A Winter Voyage." *Kaatskill Life* Vol. 18, No. 3 (Fall 2003).

———. "The Red Chasm." *Kaatskill Life* Vol 17, No.1 (Spring 2002).

Turco, Peggy. *Walks and Rambles in the Western Hudson Valley.* Woodstock, Vt.: Backcountry Publications, 1996.

Van Diver, Bradford. *Roadside Geology of New York.* Missoula, Mont.: Mountain Press Publishing Company, 1985.

Van Zandt, Roland. *The Catskill Mountain House.* Hensonville, N.Y.: Black Dome Press Corp., 1993.

Vedder, J. Van Vechten. *History of Greene County, New York, 1651-1800.* Reprint, Saugerties, N.Y.: Hope Farm Press, 1985.

Wadsworth, Bruce & The Schenectady Chapter of the Adirondack Mountain Club. *Guide to Catskill Trails: Catskill Region.* The Adirondack Mountain Club, Inc., 1988.

Wapner, Kenneth. *Catskill Rambles.* Woodstock, N.Y.: The Overlook Press, 1992.

Weinman, Steve. *A Rock with a View: Trails of the Shawangunk Mountains.* New Paltz, N.Y.: Steve Weinman, 1995.

White, Carol & David White. *Catskill Day Hikes for All Seasons.* Lake George, N.Y.: Adirondack Mountain Club, Inc., 2002.

White, Carol & David White, eds. *Guide to Catskill Trails 8.* Lake George, N.Y.: Adirondack Mountain Club, Inc., 2002.

Wiltse, Leah Showers. *Pioneer Days in the Catskill High Peaks: Tannersville and the Region Around.* Hensonville, N.Y.: Black Dome Press Corp., 1999.

Wood, Leslie C. *Holt! T'Other Way!* Middletown, N.Y.: by author, 1950.